The PUFFING PARSON

BRANCH LINE MINISTRY

*To the Gloucestershire, Warwickshire Steam
Railway and especially, Winchcombe station.
They have helped me to preserve my sanity.*

*Main front cover image: Malcolm Ranieri.
Image of son Mark, and grandsons Joel and Nathan: Martin Upton.*

The
PUFFING PARSON

BRANCH LINE MINISTRY

DAVID CAPRON

HISTORY INTO PRINT

First published by
History Into Print, 56 Alcester Road,
Studley, Warwickshire B80 7LG in 2016
www.history-into-print.com

ISBN: 978-1-85858-350-1

A Cataloguing in Publication Record
for this title is available from the British Library.

Typeset in Baskerville
Printed in Great Britain
by 4edge Ltd.

CONTENTS

ACKNOWLEDGEMENTS

With Special thanks to my family Hilary, Mark, Peter and Stephen, to the Reverend Brian Mason (Stationmaster) and to the staff of the Rother House medical practice in Stratford upon Avon and especially to Dr. Hutchinson (Member of GWSR), Dr. King, Dr. Mahmood, Dr. Khan and Nurse Sally.

FOREWORD

by Revd James Warren, Vicar of Shottery and Temporary Associate Priest
of St Nicholas and St Barnabas, Kenilworth

In his previous book, The Fiery Canon, Fr. David Capron devoted two
chapters to Shottery Parish and entertained the reader with many
stories taken from years at the 'coal face' in the Church of England. Like
St Luke, who wrote two volumes (Luke's Gospel and The Acts of the
Apostles) David has now written a sequel, and delightfully named it The
Puffing Parson.

There is a quite a sense of the theatrical in this second book: Fr. David
removes his vestments and lays them on the altar as he brings his
incumbency at St Nicholas, Alcester to an end. He signs off the Service
Register as David, Bishop Alauna (Bishop of Alcester!) With his beloved
wife, Hilary he walks hand in hand out of St Nicholas, Alcester dressed in
his best clerical suit before attending a farewell party where members of the
aristocracy, folk from his different congregations, and members of his
family mingle with Morris Dancers and local undertakers. The Puffing
Parson could be described as another Canterbury Tales: we meet attractive
ladies, monks, pilgrims, and copious barrels of local ale to say nothing of
the amazing sensitivity of the nuns of Thirsk!

There are whimsical moments but David also turns his canon's fire on
the institution of the Church of England. There are too many church
buildings, too many services, too many parishes and too many committees.
This sociable priest, who has charmed us with his colourful view of parish
life, really begins to huff and puff when he turns to the topic of the
hierarchy of the Church of England. Bishops who sit in serried ranks in the
House of Lords would be far better employed back in their dioceses
exercising their ministry to the parish clergy. After all, he asserts, the bishop
is actually 'my parish priest!'

In his final chapter, following a recent health scare, David imagines the
life of Heaven. For him it will be a steam railway, Great Western by
preference, where a cholesterol breakfast of bacon and eggs cooked on a

fireman's shovel will be available and there will be a decent real ale brewed by a micro brewery on tap. There is much here to amuse us, and David's natural vigour and energy are always apparent, but there is also another side, that of a sensitive man who has spent most of his adult life in the service of God and the Church and who has a proper respect for human beings. The interplay between this interior sensitivity and the love of performance is one of the great joys of The Puffing Parson.

INTRODUCTION

I must confess to feeling a bit of a hypocrite. When I completed *The Fiery Canon* I promised myself that I would not write a sequel. In any case I think you need to sometimes call it a day and move on. For far too long people just hang on for the sole purpose of keeping the show on the road. When I arrived at Alcester, this sort of attitude was rather prevalent; fortunately it has all but died out, but I do detect influences in some (but not all) of the villages of the Minster. I well remember telling the National President of Rotary that all that was needed was a good death, a decent burial and a glorious resurrection was bound to follow. I am glad to say that he fully appreciated what I was saying and asked if he could quote me.

I am sure you will remember Ronnie Barker. He had the humility to call it a day when he felt that he was at the top of his profession, he pulled out and ran an antiques shop in Chipping Norton. Oh, how I would love to have called and been persuaded to part with my money. Then there was Gracie Fields and her many attempts at a last bash. It really was disastrous. If it is time to go, then you should go and not hang on to experience a long drawn out and painful death.

What has drawn me to change my mind has been illness and the need to be doing something positive. Perhaps it is the age thing, but when I hit the magic 70, things started to go downhill. I did not even finish the wine at my birthday meal and then next morning found me in hospital, suffering from atrial fibrillation. It was a wakeup call and I could see the need to change my life style and to try slowing down a bit. Hence the sequel!

Those last few weeks at Alcester were very pleasant indeed and gave me the chance to work through my emotions so that they did not all come pouring out at my last service, which by then I had pencilled in as being High Mass on Sunday, January 6th 2013, The Feast of the Epiphany. In any case I wanted to enjoy the book launch of *The Fiery Canon*. I invited the Bishop of Coventry, plus the Mayor, High Bailiff and Town Crier and a glass of wine was on offer. Either Fiery Canon Rambling Sauvignon Blanc or Fiery Canon Rustic Rector's Red Merlot and I did a roaring trade.

Bishop Christopher very kindly gave a witty speech, saying that he often went to this sort of event, but noticed that when his newly published books were on sale, trade was usually very slow but today at a quick count he had worked out that there were at least 80 prospective customers trying to get into the Church House, and they had money to spend!

Well, the Town Crier cried and the Press turned up so to cut a long story short I eventually sold over 500 copies, ensuring a second print run. All very satisfying and in addition I had given away some 100 copies to family members and close friends. Now I have to live with the reality that there are no more books to go on sale and there are no more requests from punters for the book. Perhaps this is a lesson in humility which I should have learned long ago. The next few pages may well be very revealing to me!

I had decided that I should formally retire at midnight on December 31st. I had asked if the bell ringers would mind if I went up with them when they rang in the New Year. There would be a good bit of symbolism for my wife Hilary and myself. I would climb the tower as Rector but descend as a retired priest, but at least there was a free party on offer and in that respect, nothing had changed.

There had been certain legalities to observe. Bishop Christopher had confirmed my appointment as an Honorary Canon Emeritus of Coventry Cathedral, so that meant a formal letter and then the Diocesan Secretary, Simon Lloyd, needed to issue me with a licence to occupy the parsonage until we finally moved out. Then came the last funeral, last baptism and finally the last wedding which took place on Boxing Day and related to a well established Alcester Family. It appeared that the great grandparents had been married in St. Nicholas Church exactly 90 years previously. To cap it all, this particular wedding took place on a Wednesday and so at the very last moment I had been able to complete my wedding list and be able to say that I had officiated at a wedding on every day of the week.

I celebrated my last Midnight Mass and then looked forward to January 6th. Hilary had very wisely said that we should go out and enjoy ourselves, and it was very good advice indeed. My eldest son Mark was Deacon and Joel my grandson was boat boy. We had chosen the hymns together and I had put in a special request to Malcolm Proctor my organist for the *Marche Pontificale* by Widor. Biblical scholarship has recently given vent to the idea of a priest exercising some sort of Episcopal authority within a group of churches and I for one had no problem with this new line of thinking, so I rather cheekily practised a special and final signature in the service register to sign off with + David Alauna. In other words David, Bishop of Alcester! Alauna being the Latin translation. I got away with that. The service went well and I believe that there were close on 220 communicants. Before we started, I presented Hilary with 12 red roses, because there is a tradition in the more catholic churches, that at a priest's First Mass, he gives his mother 12 red roses. I could not run to that all those years ago and my mother had to make do with carnations.

I censed the high Altar at the introit and then with Joel at my side proceeded to sprinkle everyone in church with Holy water. Three Rural Deans and an Archdeacon received especially generous treatment in this respect.

I preached from the pulpit which I very rarely did and after the communion, I washed the feet of Mark, the family stripped the Nave Altar and I went up to the High Altar to kneel before the Blessed Sacrament with Mark. I then removed my Eucharistic vestments and soutane and laid them on the altar rails in the best tradition of Newman. The clerical suit was slipped on and I went back down to deliver my very last blessing and to say that it was all over now and time to say goodbye, but not before a full apostolic blessing incorporating most of the saints of England, Wales, Scotland and Ireland, plus the biblical saints and the founders of the great religious orders. Hilary and I then walked out, arm in arm. It was all very moving. Then we all walked down to St. Benedict's School for the reception and draughts of a special real ale.

However, I have forgotten to mention one thing and that was the march up the High Street before High Mass. I have always said that one should be prepared to carry one's cross at all times and so determined that I would do that same thing on the feast of the Epiphany. I persuaded the Alcester Victoria Silver Band to turn out for me. That was quite easy, the promise of a bottle of rum and a bottle of brandy to lace hot coffee, proved to be irresistible. Then there was the Colour Party of the Warwickshire Fire Brigade, which was my dad's old brigade, of which he was the Chief Officer. You may well tell me that I should be using the politically correct title of 'Fire and Rescue Service', but quite honestly, you cannot teach a leopard to change his spots and I do rather like the sound of the word 'Brigade'!

To all these parties, could be added members of the Alcester Court Leet and various recovering drunks from the night before. We started at the Fire Station and I managed to purloin the crown of thorns to be dangled over the processional cross and we came up the High Street in fine form. I had a discussion with the Police who just wanted to satisfy themselves as to what exactly was going on. The Town Clerk who was a former Churchwarden asked me if I was going to ask permission from the District Council. I told him I had determined not to trouble them as they would probably say "No" and take a long time to get there. "Good idea" he said. The Police were more than happy and chuckled over the phone, telling me that as it was not a formal affair and they had not been requested by the District Council to provide any cover, however, local intelligence had told them of certain things going on and not to worry, they would not be far away.

I had been asked by the Band as to my favourite music and my choice for this sort of event was to be the *Pomp and Circumstance March* by Elgar; *No. 4* and not *Land of Hope and Glory*, which I cannot abide and reckon to be pure institutionalised jingoism!!! Anyway, it was great and after suitable refreshments, I prepared myself to enter my church for the last time, making sure that I referred to it as the Metropolitan Cathedral Church of St. Nicholas!

So, back to the reception at the School where there were presentations and speeches. In addition I had provided a barrel of specially brewed real ale by Hobson's Brewery of Cleobury Mortimer. In fact I had persuaded the brewery to produce 12 barrels which were then liberally passed around the pubs of Alcester. I am pleased to report that all the barrels were empty by the end of the week!

Then there were invitations to supper and also another party in the Town Hall so that I could say goodbye to members of the Minster. We had some singing and also the services of the Morris Dancers who were persuaded to come along with the simple expedient of the promise of even more ale. I managed to convince some of the Undertakers to come along. They are a good crowd and can always be relied upon to provide plenty of laughter. If you ever get an invitation to an Undertaker's Hop, then have no qualms about going, you will be well looked after and will have the time of your life.

I have often fooled myself as to who gets on with me and who doesn't. It was many years ago, that I had a big bust up with the Court Leet. The

Court Leet is the Ancient Baronial Court of the Marquess of Hertford. It no longer has any legal authority, but naturally our cousins from across the seas would die for something like this back home in Uncle Sam. There is a High Bailiff and a Low Bailiff, a Constable, Brook Watcher, Flesh Taster, Bread Weigher and the most popular position on the Court which is that of Ale Taster. At the end of the year, the High Bailiff formally opens the Mop and the ancient Charter is formally read out. It all looked very good and I was looking forward to a long and mutually prosperous relationship when one Sunday I was at the High Altar, celebrating the Holy Mysteries for the 8.00am Brigade of Faithful ones when I heard this increasingly irritating and sharp tapping outside, just like Woody Woodpecker, except that it was members of the Court Leet outside shinning up a ladder at the same time as attaching coloured bunting to nails and screws.

I was incandescent with fury at what I perceived to be a typically intrusive and insensitive action by the secular members of society. I demanded to see the High Bailiff and Court Leet members on the Church Green for what was going to be a dressing down. Fortunately for me I ensured that one or two folk knew that after the dressing down, I would be dispensing plentiful libations of real ale in the Holly Bush. I was subsequently told by one of my wardens, who was a former High bailiff, that was one of the best things that I did on the community front.

So, I am sure you can well imagine both my surprise and delight to be invited by the Court Leet to be their guest on the Severn Valley Railway for a day, together with Hilary, Peter and Stephen. About fifty people filled a coach and off to Kidderminster we went where I was to be further delighted at the sight of a specially constructed headboard entitled "The Fiery Canon". It had been attached to an Ivatt Class 4; 2–6–0 loco which has lived on the SVR for most of its heritage life. The surprises did not stop there. I had been given a footplate pass and when we were out of sight of the inspector and the signalman, I actually drove the engine. She was certainly very lively, but what a thrill when having just crossed the Queen Victoria Bridge, I was able to hit the regulator and she powered up the hill in quite majestic fashion, accompanied by three blasts of her whistle. I drove her into Highley Station and then handed over control. A visit to the museum was an interesting diversion and then it was off to Bridgnorth where there was an Ale Tasting. Finally we returned to Kidderminster where there were photographs by MY ENGINE and I was then presented with the headboard which has adorned my study wall ever since.

Not quite finished yet. We needed to return to Alcester where a welcome hot stew was served up in the Town Hall. More speeches and the presentation of a scale model of a Hall Class "Ragley Hall" which would eventually run on our soon to be re-constructed model railway. Perhaps there is something to be said for delivering the occasional dressing down after all?

Chapter 1

THE MOVE

We actually moved out of the Parsonage on Tuesday February 19th, but to where? Well, it may not be known, but on resignation of the freehold of a parish, the incumbent also resigns the freehold of his parsonage and therefore must leave. In the event of death, the widow is given six months to sort out her affairs and then she must leave. It does sound a bit hard, but in fairness to the Church of England, in most cases the diocesan secretary will have been around with a decent cheque, whereby the widow will be able to get herself started in a new house.

On the face of it, there should be no problem if we had decided to buy a house in Alcester and retire there. But, it is not the done thing really and would be viewed with suspicion. You are expected to leave the parish and go away so that you cannot possibly interfere with the ministry of your successor. That is all very well if you are keen to take up pastures new, but what if you do not have much money and housing is relatively cheap in your old parish? I have known this to happen and the authorities have huffed and puffed, but in the end there was nothing they could do. I picked up a mutter from within another diocese that a threat was issued to deny a priest a permission to officiate letter, whereby he could carry on exercising a priestly ministry. It was pointed out that under European legislation, this was deemed to be illegal as it was tantamount to a restriction of free access to employment etc.

There are arguments on both sides. I for one would not want to interfere, quite honestly there comes a time when it is the correct thing to move on. I have heard some horrendous stories, but I have also heard of some priests who refused to be brow beaten, because at the end of the day, they had their own friends close by and did not see why they should be made to sacrifice them. They bought a new house in their old parish, moved in and had nothing to do with parish worship or ministry at all. There was nothing that could be done.

I would have hoped that priestly sensitivity would prevail, but I have to note with great regret that many a priest says one thing and then does the other. Not good at all! If you are in a large town then it is easier, the problems arise when you are out in the country and there is nowhere else to go. Having made your move, you then need to be clear as to the terms upon which you might go back. It does sound rather like a spy thriller, doesn't it? I kept out of Alcester for some considerable time. Part of the problem is the fact that it is a very vibrant community and you are soon seen. If I needed to pop back for a good reason, I would make sure that my successor knew, rather than he be told by someone else, who would be pleased to score some brownie points. But at the end of the day, it is all about the Church of England being the established church of the land. Everything is encompassed and bound up by the law of the land. There are times when it would appear that you need to have permission to think, let alone pray.

We eventually purchased a house in Shottery and completed on the feast of St. Andrew, November 30th, but what extra work did we need to consider?

In fact the decision was very straightforward. As far as general building work was concerned we both wanted Steve and his son in law, Adam. Steve had been District Commissioner of Scouts and had actually warranted me as a Beaver Scout Leader in my own church some years previously. Plumbing and sanitaryware could be nobody other than Pat whose wife worshipped with me regularly in Alcester and as far as decorating was concerned it just had to be Shurv from Leamington Spa with whom I had played rugby in days of yore and who had come to my ordination and First Mass. With all that sorted we could now turn to our last Christmas and make plans for the actual move.

I was especially grateful to the Diocese of Coventry and Simon Lloyd the Diocesan Secretary for agreeing to pay our removal costs. It certainly made a difference.

It is on these occasions that I needed strong support to lean on and that support was supplied by Hilary. She organised everything, right down to the smallest detail with military precision and the move was completed very smoothly. I just could not have coped!

So, the big day eventually dawned upon us and the weather was extremely clement. It is not a long journey from Alcester to Stratford upon

Avon, but the two communities are very different. We had taken the opportunity to carry over various items of gardening and potted plants etc so at least there was some visible colour on the actual day. It is surprising how many former parishioners still lived in the same road and so there were a lot of very friendly faces about. Another friendly face appeared and it was that of the Reverend Brian Mason who is a Methodist Minister and very active voluntary worker on the Gloucester Warwickshire Railway (GWR). Needless to say, by the end of the following week, I had joined up and about a month later I attended an induction course for those who wanted to volunteer on the railway.

Our two younger sons came round in the evening to help and we settled down to the traditional fish and chip supper. Next day, Virgin Media turned up as promised and we were soon in communicado with the rest of the world. There then followed the usual moving in experience of searching for lost connections etc. Correspondence turned up, so we did not have to bother the Royal Mail and then there was the important matter of arranging a House Blessing. The best way to deal with this was to invite James the vicar to come down on that first Sunday evening with his wife and also the Churchwardens and to celebrate a House Eucharist on the dining room table and then to stay behind for supper and drinks.

This worked extremely well and a good time was had by all. We both felt that our home had now been set aside for some special purpose. And so the next morning brought half term to a close and Hilary went back to work in Alcester and I found myself alone and having to cope with a new way of doing things.

So, what was I to do? Well, I had a look at the Shottery Village Association and as it needed a new chairman, I volunteered. I could also see the need for a Railway Group which might support the GWR; needless to say, I soon became chairman of that organisation. I could still contribute a little towards the diocesan cricket team by virtue of general secretarial arrangements and trying to persuade the Church Times to make some radical changes in the framework of the annual competition.

In addition of course there were opportunities to assist James at Shottery and I was only too keen to help out and give him the occasional break which he so richly deserved.

It is odd going back to a previous parish and taking a service, there will be old and familiar faces, but hopefully there will also be the interspersion of new and eager ones. You have to get the balance correct. Too much of the old faces and clearly there has been no progress. Too many of the eager beavers and obviously there has been a big bust up with the locals who have taken umbrage and left. Who would be a Priest?

Fortunately I did not have too much of a problem and there was a good balanced mixture. I remember laying out basic principles by saying that I was the old Vicar and that there was a young Vicar who lived next door. If people had problems then they went to the young Vicar as the old Vicar wanted out, they got the message!

Then there was the first funeral and the first wedding. I soon realised that I had been out of regular action for too long and was losing my grip. I needed to look up the book and annotate my paper copy so that I got things right. Even then I was making mistakes, admittedly not howlers, but certainly not acceptable to me when I was in full time ministry. Oh what it is to grow old! Lord, give me grace to smile!

But then, new channels open themselves up at unlikely times and places. I had not realised that a parish pilgrimage to Walsingham had been booked, so I soon had my name down and this led to discussions about pilgrimage in general and its relevance amongst contemporary church life.

The next stage of development was to get involved in the business of arranging a day Pilgrimage to one of the great Cathedrals. I enjoy helping out in this aspect and to date we have had really good visits to both Gloucester and Lichfield. However this did give me an idea of arranging a series of mini evening pilgrimages around the local churches whereby we could visit and receive a spiritual guide to the church, have some quiet time and then say together a Pilgrimage Litany, before adjourning to a local pub for supper. This has proved remarkably successful and allows some people to get out after work and enjoy some Christian fellowship.

But to be brutally honest when it comes to the crunch, I still think that the best decision that I made when I retired was that of joining the Gloucester Warwickshire Railway and becoming a volunteer and that is where I would like to turn my attention now. *The Fiery Canon* is about to become *The Puffing Parson* and his ramblings around the Cotswold Countryside are due to be carried out on rails and not on roads or footpaths.

Chapter 2

THE GLOUCESTERSHIRE
WARWICKSHIRE RAILWAY

I am not sure what it is about railways and especially steam heritage railways which attracts clergy, but something does and they are like bees around a honey pot. I had hoped for biblical warrant but I am not too sure if Isaiah Chapter 6 verse 4 would satisfy, especially if he or she is not of a High Church disposition!

Great names are still talked about in almost reverential tones such as Rev Awdry of *Thomas the Tank Engine* fame, Bishop Eric Treacy the noted photographer who died on Appleby Railway Station waiting for "Evening Star" to pull in and of course the irrepressible Canon Teddy Boston and his own private parsonage railway in the grounds of Cadeby Rectory. But there are others and plenty of them too. The GWR is no exception to the divine rule.

I almost managed to combine both church and railway at Stratford upon Avon on one occasion when I sat in the foyer of the Arts Centre before a production of the *Titfield Thunderbolt* by a local drama group. The railway had sponsored the production and our logo appeared on all pamphlets etc, so I put on my clericals and distributed goodwill and free brochures etc but without a bishop. Incredibly I remember the programme being filmed in Woodstock all those years ago.

However, my time with GWR is spread across all sorts of faculties, so to speak, which gives me the opportunity to speak to many varied people who enjoy just going out on the railway. Like them, I have to remember that I am a volunteer and so for the most part are all others, ensuring the smooth running of the railway. It came to me the other day that the Church of England is a voluntary society and it is very difficult to give orders and yet the good old C of E engenders much love and affection. So do Heritage Railways and in engendering that love and affection they are the instigators of much passion. Now there is nothing wrong with a bit of passion (of whatever sort) but sometimes there are no safety valves and all of a sudden there is an almighty explosion and people are hurt. When they are hurt they really are hurt, their life just ebbs away and they leave. This is a great shame as so often there is no going back and they become very lonely. It was just over a little piece of apparent nothingness which very quickly grew disproportionately until it became too late. Bang!

It is easy to be wise after the event, but I remember being taught "Sensitivity" at Theological College. They were lessons well taught and well received. Why do some people have to be bulls in china shops? And while I am on the subject, why is communication so bad in this world? It is easy to criticise, especially when volunteers cheerfully take on more responsibility. You don't have to write a long letter, Good God, we use more than enough paper nowadays, but a quick phone call or e-mail is probably all that is needed.

Quite honestly nobody is expecting a red carpet each and every time, but the reality of basic information is surely not unreasonable? And yet, I have made these simple mistakes myself, we all do don't we? Perhaps we need someone who is available to support people in these times, to rub them down and then to build them up. Every volunteer that I see on the GWR is worthy of being built up.

As far as trains in general are concerned, like many others, my interest goes back a long way. I am told that when in my pram, I used to get quite heated when a Great Western engine pulled into Minehead Station, I used to rock the pram so violently that articles fell out, but fortunately, not me.

Then there was the time that we lived in Woodstock and joy of joys the terminus of the branch line from Kidlington was situated adjacent to the primary school. The station was called Blenheim and Woodstock, but then with the Duke of Marlborough living just up the road in his modest detached Versailles look alike Palace, that was understandable. Midweek, you changed at Kidlington if you wanted to get to Oxford, but on Saturdays the trip took on halcyon proportions and it was a through train to the City of Dreaming Spires. Needless to say, all good things are subject to the vagaries of human beings and the line was closed with much traditional trumpeting, whistles, detonators etc. I remember it well. March 1st 1954 was the final day and I still have a ticket issued on the penultimate day.

We ultimately moved to Rugby, which I thought was in the northern command with smoke and dirt etc. Amazingly, during my relatively short time there, the main line from Euston was electrified and Rugby was considered to be in the Home Counties and well within the commuter belt. But Rugby had one great advantage over most other towns and cities, that was its facilities for train spotting!

Rugby (Midland) Station was much favoured because there were lines to London with an alternative via Northampton, also to Birmingham and Glasgow with smaller lines extending their tentacles to Leicester, Market Harborough and Leamington Spa. But you were not finished there, because at the end of the 19th century, the Great Central Railway decided to drive southwards to Marylebone in London and chose Rugby as the point of crossover with the various Midland railways. What a place to train spot! There was this small field which nobody seemed to own and it was as close to the railway as you could possibly desire. My favourites were the Stanier Pacifics which came through "like a knife through butter" and then there were the Jubilees and the Patriots and Royal Scots, Mickeys and Class 8s. Diesels made an appearance and by the time I had left school, the first of the main line electric locos had searched out Rugby.

I remember on Remembrance Sunday noticing that a loco seemed to have been specially decorated. Further investigation showed it to be the Patriot Class Leader and it had been sensitively decorated with poppies. The original "Deltic" paid us a visit as did No 10000 and 10001, also the Gas Turbine loco, No 18000. But what we really looked forward to in the very heart of Midland territory was a Friday afternoon on the Great Central at about 4.00pm when a southbound express was virtually guaranteed to be hauled by a Great Western Locomotive. Joy of joys!

My Father used to take me to Bicester North on a Friday afternoon when it was possible to see a slip coach in action; that was certainly a most interesting experience plus the occasional visit to Woodford Halse Engine Shed when the display of a ten bob note did wonders when permission was asked for a visit around the shed. I well remember 9Fs in every large nook and cranny just simmering and waiting for their next tour of duty.

I will always be grateful to my parents who encouraged this interest of mine in steam railway engines. It goes back a long way and I can still remember standing on the platform of Holkham Station in the very early 1950s, when this mighty beast came in with a train for Wells next the Sea.

If you walk down to the beach at Holkham today, there is very little left, other than a pile of stones. Norfolk has always been of interest to me as there was a profusion of lines. I am so pleased that I did actually travel on the M&GN from Peterborough to Fakenham. Needless to say it is no longer. Many will say that there was too much in the way of single track for it ever to be a really profitable line. However, holiday makers came from the east midlands in their droves and fresh fruit replaced them on the return journey. On that one journey we changed at South Lynn allowing our train to slide off down the spur into Kings Lynn. Eventually our dedicated train came in, bound for Melton Constable and I remember looking for an empty compartment for my mother and myself. I decided which compartment would be ideal for our purpose and was just about to open the door and get in when I noticed a clergyman sitting there. He looked extremely parsonical and very boring, so we nipped into the adjoining carriage instead. I am prepared to swear that I had no dreams of a clerical career at that point, in any case I was about to tolerate five years of public school religion and that was enough to put anyone off.

If you were to pin me down and request that I specify my favourite locomotives, then I cannot duck out of putting King George V at the top of the list. No 6000 with the bell at the front. My mother took me to Reading for a session of train spotting. As we came into the station we were held at the signals and as I looked out of the window I could see that the signals for the west bound main line for Cornwall had all been dropped into the "Go" position. It was 10.30 in the morning and at that moment the Cornish Riviera Express came through like a joyful greyhound, and then all was quiet and we were given permission to enter Reading station. I would put Clun Castle in second place. I have driven that loco at Tyseley Works. Admittedly not very far and only up to the rake of semaphore signals that protected the main line. I also experienced this same loco pulling the last steam hauled express on the Western Region. I was on Hatton bank at the time and it was just like being on Blackpool beach. Then a small aeroplane came in low so as to record the sound! I will not endeavour to repeat what was being said, but I think the pilot got the message and flew away! We were treated to a spectacular display of majesty and might and she mounted the bank with consummate ease. My third favourite is a narrow gauge engine called "Russell" which now resides at Porthmadog on the old Welsh Highland Railway. When the WHR went into liquidation she had quite a colourful existence and for a time found employment in the iron ore quarries of Hook Norton. Eventually she returned and was greeted tearfully by her old driver who was beside himself with emotion.

I only ever saw King George V twice whilst in service and the last time was in the final days of steam at Wolverhampton Low Level Station when I was on the other platform and this rather grubby loco puffed into the London platform. It was only when I saw a bell at the front that I recognised the loco to end all locos. It was tipping down with rain, but I stood outside and away from the platform canopy for that last look and then what we all want to hear, the actual departure with all the regal splendour possible.

Those many years later when I had become ordained and decided to go up north, I became aware of a different sort of splendour. This was more down to earth, more basic, more austere at times, but still splendid. These were the many railways of the North East. At the end of the day, it is no exaggeration to say that they were born up there and certainly the locals are very proud of what is a splendid inheritance.

Being a Somerset man, I had to be very careful that I did not mix up certain initials, especially the S & D. In Somerset, it is the Somerset and Dorset Railway, in Durham it is the Stockton and Darlington Railway. Both are very different, both suffered from political interference of some sort or other and one has been erased from the map and exists only in memory. At least I can tune into that memory because when I was at Wells Theological College all those years ago, I happened to be walking up on Maesbury Summit and my friend could not resist saying that he thought he could hear a couple of 9Fs pulling the Pines Express!! The Somerset and Dorset had made the mistake of criss crossing Great Western territory; a sin for which it would ultimately pay the supreme price of extinction. The opportunity presented itself when after nationalisation in 1948, the various regions were re-arranged and the Western Region found itself responsible for the Somerset and Dorset. Joys unbounded! It was then easy to ensure a timetable which was neither use nor ornament to anyone, leading to the inevitable decision to close a line which nobody was actually using.

The Stockton and Darlington was a product of its locality, whereby it enabled coal which was close to the surface to be hauled to the coast. The problem was always going to be the local landowners who being part of the establishment did not want new fangled machinery spoiling their quiet and prosperous life. Fox hunting was more important and in any case was it really necessary for the lower classes to be encouraged to ask for passenger coaches so that they could get around? The aristocracy could see what the logical conclusions would be to a railway for the transportation of coal. Others look at this in a different light and it took the combined efforts of local Roman Catholics and Quakers to force it through. But operate it did and although perhaps it could never quite match the Liverpool and Manchester Railway, I can still say that everything started on that September day in 1825 at the Masons Arms in Shildon and the world has not seen the like of it since. I have always contented myself with the fact that it lay in my parish of Newton Aycliffe and it was the world's first public steam hauled railway that carried passengers. I even took my Beaver colony out for a trip on the line. You should have seen the Ticket Collector's face when I asked for 24 return children's tickets!

Chapter 3

EARLY DAYS AS A VOLUNTEER

The first thing that you do as a volunteer (other than sign an application form) is to attend an Induction morning at the railway headquarters. When you have completed the morning session, you are presented with your temporary work permit. There can be no getting away from this at all. We may well be volunteers, but that is no justification for an amateurish approach and just "playing" at trains. At the end of the day we are running a railway and all sorts of safeguards need to be learned about and understood. Safety is paramount and cannot be compromised in any way. Having worked for a few years as an Insurance Claims Adjuster, I can reassure you that Insurance Underwriters are more than a little fussy when it comes down to Liability Insurance and who can blame them?

I had determined that initially I would do a little portering on the platforms and commence my career as a Meeter and Greeter. Portering was very enjoyable and I would go along to Toddington with Brian Mason and just generally help out, in most cases this meant the imparting of information about train times. It pays to have a timetable handy, helping elderly folk cross the line was also of prime importance and naturally you always wore a high viz jacket on these occasions. Another task was changing the times of trains board and also remembering to put up the correct colour for the type of timetable that was operating on that day.

However, meeting and greeting provided me with much fun and the opportunity to talk in depth about the railway if necessary. You did not have the worry of where all your customers were because they were safely on the train. Generally speaking though, I found that many people were just happy to watch the world go by and reminisce about the old times of steam, smoke and smuts! But, I did learn very quickly that one of the first things you did when your coach party arrived was to show them all where the toilets were and then to fish out he or she with the money and guide them to the ticket office. First things first, of course.

On these trips there are reserved seats and as this puts your customers together, it's fairly easy to talk to them if required. In the summer it can get quite crushed, so when everyone gets out at Cheltenham racecourse to sniff the fresh air, you need to stick around, because if you don't, the reserved seats will be occupied by usurpers, irrespective of the liberal distribution of reserved notices. Another good ploy is to load yourself up with brochures covering future special events. These go down very well and rest assured there are boxes and boxes of them at Toddington. I usually finish off by handing out brochures to all and sundry, especially the time-tables because I find that grandparents have this habit of wanting to take their grandchildren on the trains. The saying of good-bye is just as important as the welcome. A cheerful wave does not cost anything, plus the fact that you see the reassuring smiles of a coach load of satisfied customers who will tell their families and their neighbours that they have had a wonderful day out on the friendly Cotswolds Line. Last but not least, don't forget to wear your uniform! White shirt, black shoes, dark blazer, jacket, tie and any appropriate badges. Smiling is free of charge for all.

Now that I had bitten the bullet so to speak, I was looking for other new pastures down at the railway and as it was coming up to Christmas, the possibility of being a Santa, presented itself. I had a particular interest in Santa as my last church was dedicated to St. Nicholas and there is a strong tradition that the two persons are in fact just one. I was amused by all the paperwork that came out. Very important. I have no problem in the authorities laying down the law, especially when there are children involved. The funny bit was the instruction that in no way should any child be dangled on a Santa knee for photographs etc, unless the mother expressed a very strong determination that this should happen, HOWEVER, if a mother or even a grandmother wished to be dangled on a Santa knee then the organisers were not going to interfere!! Guess what, I attracted the attentions of a very delightful grandma! Big girl, I was almost squashed!

The whole Santa enterprise is extremely well organised, even down to putting all the presents onto a three year computer cycle. Winchcombe is an ideal half way house. The suitably decorated train arrives and children are escorted off and make their way down to the Elf Shed where they are lined up for their visit by a selection of suitably dressed elves. It is done in such a way that the children only ever see one Santa, so the entry and departure are very strictly controlled via a series of screens. In fact there are three Santas and we recline on our delightful thrones, listening to soothing and tender Christmas music. Then we are woken out of our slumbers by our individual elf announcing that she has one or two children for us – sometimes more, I once had a virtual tribe! Now for the speedy bit, because you just under two minutes per child. I always suggest that the parents start off with photographs, otherwise they get forgotten, then a quick play with some of the toys, followed by a question as to what the child would like for Christmas, a few loud Ho Hos! And then its present time and a question to the parents as to age determines which coloured bag the child takes hold of. If there are problems we are ready to change or swop, because what we want are happy children. There is even a little present when a bump presents itself! The happy family then departs; I re-adjust my beard and await my next customer.

In my first year I had a family from Mexico, also Hungary, Australia and the States. Eventually you have a break between a train departing and the next arriving, when you can do a strip off and relax with a coffee, we also take it in turns to run along the side of the platform as the train departs and wave to the children, but be careful, some of them are very sharp eyed and can determine whether you were their actual Santa. One year I had five Chinese ladies and that was great fun, especially when it came to sitting on knees and photographs. It was a hen party and some of them had flown in from China to join up with their friends. An apparent problem as to what present they might like was instantly resolved when it transpired that they all were more than happy with a dolly. I felt that I had done my bit for Sino British relations.

I also remember during my first session, welcoming into my grotto a well-built father with his family. Of ruddy complexion, he looked as if he came from the farming community and when he opened his mouth to speak, I was sure he came from God's own country! Somerset. Land of the fermented juice of the apple, and I was right. While his children played with the toys and had their photographs taken, I was able to slip in a question as to where he came from? "You wouldn't know it," he said rather loftily. "Try me," I said. "Chewton Mendip" said he. "Preached my first sermon there," said I, "and then went in the pub for an assessment." The pub is still there, I was told. What is interesting here is that this family came all the way up from south of Bristol and were regular customers. We must be doing something right despite some people making out all is not as it should be.

I had this problem when I was a full time parish priest. I found that parishioners were dragging their own church down, we don't do this and we don't do that etc. I got so fed up one day, that I halted the meeting and got out a piece of paper. I then asked for details of all the things that we were doing in the parish that were good! I soon needed more paper. It is so easy to talk ourselves off the planet and I have heard exactly the same moans on the Railway. I had a delightful compliment paid by a member of the SVR the other day. He just said "You have a lovely Railway."

Wartime in the Cotswolds is a great experience. Everyone enjoys dressing up and I can assure you that the clergy are no exception. Interestingly, as it is a wartime commemoration then naturally service uniforms are prevalent but I did notice that very few dressed as "other ranks" officer gear was the order of the day! I had a lot of fun, but there are a many pit holes to avoid. It is the old stories of certain people have always done certain things and heaven forbid if you interfere. As I have said before, I am all for a certain amount of healthy independence, but what are we doing this for?

The delightful thing about Winchcombe is that it is the half way point and passengers leave the trains to explore and sample our delights. There are few parking facilities and it is much easier to come by train. We can offer Real Ale, courtesy of the local brewery from just down the road. We can offer an original and authentic air raid, including a V1 to finish off with. We can also offer Morris dancing and of course we can offer wartime singing. All in all, very good value for money and there is the train journey too.

If you fancy dressing up, then do not feel restricted to service gear. A regular customer comes all dressed up as an Undertaker including a measuring tape around his neck. I greeted him with the inevitable welcome of "Yours eventually". He even danced on the platform and I am hoping that he will return each year.

Winchcombe is ideal for other activities too and the Schools Wartime Evacuation Days are great fun. I remember opening up Winchcombe station one morning together with Brian Mason and Claudette Oddy. Interestingly we are all ordained, Anglican, Methodist and Baptist, in that order. Claudette happened to mention that the Evacuation group could do with some more helpers so I made contact and turned up to understudy one of the regulars. Again this is a wonderful opportunity for children to experience what happened all those years ago. Many of the schools go to incredible lengths to prepare their pupils and they dress up and also make gas masks to give it that authentic touch. There are usually three farmers to greet them all suitably dressed with our own special artefacts. I carry a Bishop's Crozier which gives me the opportunity to be a Shepherd and in any case I can then control the inevitable rush to cross over the bridge. The first thing is to give a safety briefing and then to point out that when the children pass onto the platform, they are going back about 75 years, to the time of their grandparents and when there was not much in the way of basic services, let alone computers, mobiles and flash cars. Once on the platform, we await the arrival of the train.

Now, all was going well with these sorts of trips which could easily be justified by schools as being well within the key stage 2 history remit. Then the government decided to change the rules which meant that on the face of it these trips could not be justified. Needless to say, there were howls of protest from across the Heritage Railway Movement as we were talking about a very significant loss of revenue. In the end it would appear that a compromise of sorts was reached and the trips continued much to the delight of the children, the financial departments of the railways and last but not least, the teachers, for whom it was a glorious introduction into creative writing.

Back on the train, and the excitement of finding your place, and settling everyone down. The experience covers a trip to Cheltenham racecourse and return. The stopover at Cheltenham enables the children to experience some watering of the engine, disconnection, run round and reconnection. Occasionally, if they are lucky they can have the briefest of visits to the footplate itself, but then the whistle goes and we chuff off back to Winchcombe. However the train trip is not just a question of admiring the beautiful scenery, but it is a good opportunity to learn some old fashioned wartime songs, such as, *White Cliffs of Dover* and *Pack up your troubles* etc. Professional Musicians who are members of the GWR lead this part of the morning and while this is going on, the other half of the children settle down to listening to wartime evacuation stories from elderly members who were in London at the time of the Blitz.

It doesn't take long before we arrive back in Winchcombe, this time on platform 2 and right into the waiting arms of the Fire Department who are all dressed up in A.F.S. Uniform and ready to train the children in fire fighting techniques. There are not many dry children at the end of this exercise.

The fun really starts towards the end of the fire drill. I am hovering outside the waiting room on Platform 2 with David Brown who has set up a magnificent recording of an air raid, together with warning sirens and all clear sirens. Once the children have all had a go at both carrying water in old cloth buckets and also squirting water and/or pumping it, we arrange for the air raid siren to start up. It is distinctive and so we hurry the children into the waiting room and close the door. All is dark, other than a couple of flickering candles. Usually there is some upset and occasionally, some screaming, especially when we tell them that they might be in there for up to 6 hours and of course the toilet arrangements are basic, to say the least.

These recordings are the pride and joy of David Brown and he has put a lot of work into it. We understand that we are unique in providing this facility, although it would not surprise me if other railways decided to do the same in the very near future.

But, back to the raid! The farmer has a small torch, just in case, but that is it and the children have to settle down for a good ten minutes of ack ack guns, bombs, planes crashing and our *piece de resistance* which is an attack by a Doodlebug (V1). We tell the children to count to 5 once the doodlebug stops making a noise. We tell them that at this point, the flying bomb is tumbling to earth. It might hit us, it might not! Then there is a big crash and the 'all clear' siren sounds. At this point a crowd of youngsters excitedly, and yet very relieved, exit fairly smartly.

Dependent on the timetable, this is usually when the children have lunch and a bit of a run around to let off any excess steam. Once the picnic area has been tidied up, the children are regaled by Mollie who is a true Londoner (with accent) who tells them what it was like to be evacuated as schoolchildren. She is quite a character and does not take prisoners. We all have to behave ourselves; especially the adults and we dare not talk! But we do have to put our lives at risk by endeavouring to stop Mollie in full flight. She is absolutely great but we do have to do other things and so we have learned to give the secret sign about ten minutes before we need to move onto the next activity.

The children usually finish off their day out by going to the Elf Centre and learning about all those domestic artefacts that were used in those days. A darning mushroom is always a source of fascination as are the small squares of newspaper, threaded together and which hang up in the outdoor toilet. The girls soon pick up the skipping ropes and the boys settle down to a game of marbles; they usually spill out onto the platform and the scene is a picture of utter contentment. The point is made that such joy and happiness is provided through some very simple and cheap artefacts.

We are almost there, and all that remains to be done is for a final gathering and decision on who is going to take on what job at the farm to which they have been sent... Some jobs are more popular than others, naturally and the gender gap is still fairly pronounced. The girls go for milking and horses, whereas the boys want to drive tractors and the like, having said that it does not take long before all the jobs are taken and it is time to say good- bye. As they pass off the platform into the yard we tell them that now it is back to the modern world and suddenly they have jumped 75 years. Their modern coach awaits them.

Chapter 4

SOME EARLY REFLECTIONS ON
MINISTRY, PAST, PRESENT AND FUTURE

Well, the good old Church of England is still around. By some sort of Johannine miracle it can still be seen operating in most townships and villages. It must have some special hidden fuel, because quite honestly it really should have gone to the wall years ago. If it was being operated as a business, then it just would not survive. It is a typical voluntary society, amongst many. Naturally there are some historical reasons for where it finds itself in the strata of society, but when it comes down to the crunch, the Church of England has too many churches, too many services, too many parishes and too many committees. At the very least it needs to drag itself away from the standard quip, that when the C of E finds it has a problem, it immediately forms a committee! What that committee actually does, is a totally separate issue. By virtue that the C of E is the established church of the nation, it is established by law and therefore has bound itself into a cocoon of immovability. There is a good argument for an established church and there are equally compelling arguments as to why we should not have one.

The Church loves to talk and talk incessantly. There are exhilarating reports in the ecclesiastical press about exciting debates on Synod. On the face of it we are very fortunate to be living within the tentacles of a go go church. We should be very grateful for dynamic leadership and all other churches should be learning from our outstanding example. But it is not the case! The C of E suffers from a self imposed disease and that is delusion. Delusion about the reality of life around about. It is really a question of incarnation and what we mean by it. The whole business of Christ living in this world so that we might have the opportunity to both live out and share in his glory. There is much talk about preaching the gospel. But what do we mean by preaching? Perhaps I am biased, but many a good act of worship has been ruined by a long and boring sermon. St. Francis had the right idea. To preach to gospel is to live out the gospel and if you do have to preach in the traditional manner, then the fewer words the better. How refreshing!

The most important resource of the Church of England is its clergy. There seems to be a view which is becoming increasingly prevalent, that all you do is give the clergy a parsonage, some basic expenses and a whole host of services to take and you have covered your responsibilities. I do not see the point of starting up an ancient heating system for a handful of people. Yes, these country churches are beautiful, for the most part, but the refusal to worship elsewhere is a downright heresy and it is about time that someone up top told them. God is not limited to a pile of medieval stones in the middle of a field. To my mind, God is not limited and can be found in dirty cities, distant shores, mountains and valleys. I am not saying anything about closing churches down. It would not happen anyway, because English Heritage would start having a nationally inspired heart attack. But what about some sort of legal protective hibernation, whereby the church could always be used for local baptisms, weddings and funerals and perhaps a monthly service in the warmer months? Do people want stone or do they want flesh?

I can remember, Keith Arnold, the first Bishop of Warwick once saying to me that I should not worry if people tell me that I only work one day per week. Let them think it, he said. I did actually take nine services on one Sunday when I was Vicar of Shottery all those years ago. I was absolutely shattered at the end of the day and swore never to repeat the exercise. I am of the opinion that if you really put everything that you have into your sermon and into celebrating the Eucharist, then one service, or possibly two services should suffice. I can't see that going down well in the country, but those who moan ought to look at our non-conformist friends who, if there are no punters, will close a chapel down and those who come occasionally, will just have to make their way to another chapel. The trouble with the Church of England is that it has encouraged the belief that all you have to do is to walk down the main street and there will be a church awaiting your attention.

The problem today is that for the average incumbent there is a vastly increased amount of bureaucracy and paperwork, or if you prefer, computer work. It can really bog him or her down and then they have to put up with the usual moans that the vicar does not visit. What the ordinary punter does not realise is that the incumbent has to go through a long and bureaucratic procedure every time that any slight alteration is proposed to a church building. I was once told by the Diocesan Registrar that strictly speaking, even putting a jam jar with wild flowers into church involves going through a procedure called the Faculty Jurisdiction Measure. As far as buildings are concerned, it is stupid, because the church would need to go through planning procedures with the local authority, but this has to be repeated, by going through an ecclesiastical equivalent. There will always be matters of opinion, but this just does not help. At the end of the day, I played a diplomatic game and generally speaking got on well with the authorities, but I did have my moments!

This brings me back to the whole business of what incumbents do with their time. When I retired, I was responsible for eight churches in nine centres of population. Up to a point, I could cope with that all right, but then you have the Parochial Church Councils, and I had five of them and each PCC had two Church Wardens. I am all for a fulsome contribution from the laity and I am all for plenty of consultation, but quite honestly we have gone far too far and there needs to be some limitations laid down or we get nowhere. One way to start this off would be to cut down dramatically the number of PCCs, one for each town, and that would cover the villages as well. The majority shareholding, so to speak, would be held by the town, but the villages would have a specified number of places. Basically, it is where the centre of ministry is, that there needs to be the political muscle. Any PCC needs to be dynamic and we should consign to the dustbin, all those notions of churchwardens who have served their villages for 40 years, likewise members of the PCC. A system of limited periods needs to be in place and if there are no comers at the Annual Meeting, then the parish fails and is brought under the direct authority of the bishop. Howls of protest, I am sure!

The main problem with the Church of England is that with an increasing lack of resources, it is trying to fool itself by continuing to serve the countryside in an apparently similar vein. It is OK to spread the jam thinly, but there comes a time when there is no more jam to spread and people still want some. That jam has to be made available for all, but the all must be prepared to change their habits so as to have some. I remember when I was on the Diocesan Board of Finance back in the 1980s, we were being told that of all the C of E resources, approximately three quarters was being directed towards rural ministry. I wondered about all the cities and the vast urban sprawls where people lived because they actually had no alternative. I wondered about the North East where I was soon to go. It all seemed so unfair and yet coupled with this state of affairs we could still hear all the talk about mission. Corporate hypocrisy! And would you believe it, when I retired I was advised by someone in the know that those proportions had varied very little. One day, the Church of England will learn! It cannot continue to live on what is in effect, institutionalised theft. It needs to look at other churches which are not tied in any way and see how they do things.

Perhaps this is an opportunity to reflect on the ecumenical dimension of ministry which I have experienced over the years. One thing I have learned is that for there to be any fruitful endeavour, there needs to be a strong missionary dimension. As long as we avoid some of those schismatic sects which have originated for the most parts in foreign climes it would appear to be far preferable to join forces when attempting to evangelise a thumping big housing estate.

I have found that also, there are occasions which are clearly God given, when warm friendships are formed and there is a greater understanding of apparently diverging viewpoints. There is a story which may well be apocryphal of a Free Church Congregation worshipping in their little chapel at the edge of a forest. It was hymn singing time and they were feeling very much that they were in the presence of the Lord. Needless to say, the weather was absolutely abysmal. That same afternoon a Roman Catholic Church had decided to have a parish hike, but they had got themselves lost in this wood and with bad weather and darkness approaching they were beginning to get worried.

They stopped and consulted their map. Where were they? Then someone said, "I hear voices. In fact I hear singing." At the same time, one of the worshippers in the chapel happened to look out of the window and saw a group of bedraggled walkers and they were carrying a cross. Need I say more?

There was very prompt action. The hikers were virtually dragged inside and sat down. The wet clothes were torn from their bodies and hot tea was served. Arrangements were made for their coach to be contacted and just to finish off they all prayed together. Those who were there have never forgotten that occasion. Long-lasting friendships were formed and the parish priest and minister reached a very gracious understanding of their respective viewpoints. All because they lost their way and yet they found it again. Or perhaps I should say that their way was found for them. We need to recognise opportunities for ecumenical witness. That was a clear example, but there are others. I must confess that I have not been a big supporter of Councils of Churches and other sundry bodies. To my mind, they are just talking shops and do very little. The only reason that they persist is that those who sit on the top table find that this is the only opportunity for them to exercise any authority. This may seem a bit hard, but when we formed the first Local Ecumenical project in the County, the local Council of Churches was just not interested. Perhaps the fact that it was going to happen up the road in Shottery and not in Stratford upon Avon had something to do with it?

There are liturgical and theological dangers as well. I have found in some Ecumenical projects that there has been a dumbing down of just about everything that could be dumbed down. It does no good at all and leaves everyone feeling a little frustrated. When I was a curate all those years ago in Coventry I found that there was a genuine interest in how other churches operated and especially in their liturgy. I remember a particularly instructive Stations of the Cross which was put on by the local Roman Catholic Church for the benefit of the local Nonconformists and Anglicans. Mind you the local Anglicans were of the High Church variety and some of them actually practised the Stations of the Cross for their own spiritual benefit, but it was good to see the Roman Catholic priest emphasise the biblical background which of course was warmly received. Our Roman Catholic friends were able to appreciate how important the sermon was to many other Christians.

So, learning about one another is always a good thing, which leads me to the next stage. Where do we go from here?

In most cases, there is not much of a problem with baptism, although we all need to recognise that our Baptist friends do have special views on this matter. The problem is as always that of intercommunion. For many, there is no problem, and there is just an open table and yet there is sorrow when this liturgical hospitality is not offered in return. It is a difficult one isn't it? I come from the definite Anglo Catholic background, so would not be too keen on unrestricted intercommunion, but there are times when it should be offered and offered with much grace and love. I am thinking of weddings and funerals etc. What possible harm can that do? At the very least it shows a degree of Christian love and sensitivity. And yet it is sensitivity that is the key word. I have seen people trying to elbow their way into the liturgical scrum so that they can receive communion at another church. We need to be invited; it is just that these invitations are too scarce to my mind. Yes. What I believe at the consecration is probably different to others, at least we stand together and that is a witness in itself.

Chapter 5

THE RELIGIOUS LIFE IN
THE CHURCH OF ENGLAND

I must be honest and say right from the beginning that if you gave me the choice between dealing with ecumenical matters with other churches and building up connections with the Religious Communities then there is no contest. Most of my time has been naturally with Anglican foundations and generally speaking with the Franciscans. I was at Wells Theological College at the time, when the peace and tranquillity was rudely disturbed by a bevy of Franciscan Friars and Sisters. I cannot quite remember the circumstances but I can certainly remember their presence. It was absolutely inspirational. They came, they saw and they certainly conquered me. They were such great fun and yet they did not mess around when it came down to speaking out. Theirs was a radical message of the gospel. They went for the jugular every time and did not flinch. Sermons were well worth waiting for. They practised what they preached and for once in the Church of England you began to see the whole idea of going out into the highways and byways being put into practice.

Fortunately for me, their main friary and convent was not all that far away, so, together with others, I was able to maintain contact and became a Companion of the First Order of the Society of St. Francis. SSF was formed some years ago by the merger of three religious communities which were Franciscan in ethos. They are reasonably strong in this country and can also be found in Papua New Guinea, the Solomon Islands, Australia/New Zealand and the United States of America. I did look at the Tertiaries some years ago, but it was not for me. I prefer to try and live out basic Franciscan principles and have fun.

It was while I was at Theological College at Salisbury that a few of us got up at some unearthly hour in the morning and drove over to Hillfield for what is called a 'Clothing'. This is the making of a novice, when the prospective friar puts on his habit for the first time and encompasses himself with the monastic girdle with one knot. It had been a glorious drive through the Wiltshire countryside and the service was memorable as well, it took place in the chapel which is actually a converted cow barn. There were lots of benches distributed around the walls and cushions generally scattered about so as to encourage a degree of informality. Not very Anglican perhaps? But so what!

The two prospective novices turned up in open-neck shirts, jeans and sandals.

At some suitable point after the sermon, the candidates were led out into the sacristy and then returned, wearing their habits for the first time, when they also took on a new name. I remember that the two new novices were entitled, Juniper and Jacob. But I particularly remember what happened next because it literally brought the house down. There was a big friar sitting on the end of a bench and a little friar sitting on the other end. The little friar got up to assist the 'clothing ceremony' with the result that the bench shot up and the big friar slid gracefully down onto the floor. Much mirth and in typical Franciscan style, we all joined in. This sort of thing happens not too infrequently at Franciscan worship and to my mind that is no bad thing. A little bit of humour goes a long way. No boredom here!

When I was at Salisbury, it was a delight to find that one of my fellow ordinands was a fully professed Franciscan Friar, David Mason, (Bro Dominic), who had a wicked sense of humour. Like me he went home during the vacations. Home for him was Glasshampton Monastery which was about one hour's drive from where I was living at Leamington Spa. It was suggested that we meet up during the vacation for a day out plus, of course, a visit to the local pub.

My father agreed to drive and clearly was interested in what he might find. Dad was a very low church Roman Catholic, so I was not too sure how he would react. Anyway, we drove over towards the River Severn and out on the Stourport Road in the middle of some delightful countryside. The monastery is the old stable block of Great Witley Court and there is a very rough track to drive up to it. Other than some feral cats, it is very wild and remote. Muntjac deer abound, as do buzzards and the occasional peregrine falcon puts in an electrifying performance. The monastery had been inhabited by a hermit, known as William of Glasshampton. He set up the hermitage just before the war and despite being some way off the road and up quite a steep hill, people started to walk up to visit him. Nothing has really changed has it over the years? A Holy Man or a Holy Woman looking for apparent seclusion and they soon get visitors. At Glasshampton, even the local Member of Parliament turned up, mind you he was the Prime Minister – Stanley Baldwin. But that did have benefits later on when William died, because arrangements were soon made for him to be buried up there.

Anyway, we had a brief look around and then drove off to give Dominic a day out. You should have seen the look on people's faces when a fully professed Franciscan Friar in monastic habit walked into the lounge bar of the Walnut Tree in Leamington Spa! Dominic had a good day out and we returned him safely to Glasshampton later that evening. By the way, if you are thinking of taking out a friar, a monk or a nun, then just remember that they take a vow of poverty, so the drinks are on you!

Raymond Christian is another friar who I remember with great affection. It was basically, just the welcome, it was always warm and very Franciscan. He told me once that a few days after I had departed from one of my retreats, a car load of elderly ladies turned up to visit them. Unfortunately their car was too low slung and came to a halt with a horrible scraping noise. I had spent my free time swinging a pick axe and creating a trench for the surface water to run off, but unfortunately I had not done a good job and should have hammered down the surface a bit more. He could tell me many stories, such as the time when the friar on duty in the kitchen had been a cook in the Egyptian Army. Brother Seraphim produced some sumptuous dishes with African/Asian flavours. However, when he moved on, a poor novice was put on duty and unfortunately he knew nothing about cooking. I saw the end results of his endeavours. The food was sparse and splodgey and the faces of the friars were a picture! They can be quite irreverent up there and are no respectors of rank. On one occasion, the Big Boss Friar turned up. The toilets needed cleaning out so he got the job and then preached to his brothers afterwards, I could see some very wicked gleaming eyes behind spectacles.

There are quite a few Friaries in this country and I have been to many of them. I called at the main community in Dorset to see Brother Patrick on one occasion. Bro Patrick was the treasurer and had quite a fearsome reputation. It was reckoned to be easier to raid the vaults of the Bank of England than to get any money out of the Brother Treasurer. On one famous occasion, there had been a general Chapter meeting and it had been decided that one of the younger Brothers should go to Taize which is a large and well established ecumenical centre in France. No problem in that you would say, and you would be correct until the messy business of money came up. "Go and see Patrick," was the helpful suggestion, "he will look after you." "Certainly," said Patrick, "here is a pound, mind you bring back the change"! Rather different to Patrick was Robert Hugh in San Francisco, it was rather incongruous to hear his very cultivated and very English accent in the backstreets of that amazing city. I spent a day with him and it was memorable, especially the flagon of wine that was donated in time for supper.

The founding Fathers of the Franciscans made their mark in the East End of London, especially in Plaistow. Their presence there today counts for a lot and it is good to see them there and also as very much part of the local scene.

The friars are also at Alnmouth up in Northumberland. I have been a couple of times and what I particularly remember is the backdrop to the chapel, which is basically the North Sea. It is quite an imposing house, but it has a history! It transpires that it was a dance hall in the old days with a reputation for salaciousness, but then that is where I would expect to find the Franciscans today! Brother Silyn once insisted on going into a block of flats of very dubious reputation when told that wicked women were living there!

Then there was Brother Ramón! I can see that there would have been a lot of people who had found Ramón rather difficult to cope with. Such an enthusiast. I think he was a Welsh Baptist Minister who came over to Anglicanism. You knew he was around, you could not possibly miss him and yet a man of great prayer and contemplation. Eventually he decided to try his vocation as a hermit and set up at Glasshampton at the bottom of the vegetable garden. His faithful dog, Mungo could toddle down to see his master as would visiting penitents. He did a roaring trade and yet you only have to read his books to appreciate that he did live the life of a hermit who was able to commune with his Lord. Obviously there had to be some sort of communication, especially in respect of mail and basic provisions, but he lived in three huts and just went into the Friary once each year on the Feast of St. Francis for Mass. His seat in chapel was kept free for him on that day.

Ramón died on the floor of a cell with his arms outstretched in the sign of the cross, an old friend of his, a Baptist Minister, was with him. I am told that the funeral in Worcester Cathedral was impressive. His own blood sister was there and she wore white and was surrounded by (her brothers) the friars in their brown habits. His name lives on, especially with his many books and what surprised and delighted me was when I found out that he was an old friend of my Bishop, Bp Simon Barrington-Ward. In fact they had jointly published a book together themselves.

I could tell many more stories about the friars, but it is time to suggest that you make a visit to a friary. You will soon soak up the flavour of the place. There is this glorious feeling of tranquillity and you will feel very much at home in the chapel. It may appear to be a little austere, but the Friars have never thrown their money around. In their opinion, wild flowers from the hedgerows will have the desired effect. The chapel at Glasshampton can be quite stunning in its simplicity and I have spent many profitable hours there, also in the oratory which is next door.

Perhaps now is the time to move onto the female orders, where I have always been very generously welcomed. In most cases it has been a convent with a bias towards St. Benedict and the life of the community has centred on prayer and contemplation. I think the first community of that ilk would have been the Holy Name Sisters at Malvern Link (now at Duffield). I went there to place an order for a priest's cope and came into contact with a very powerful nun called Sister Elaine. She designed my cope on the back of a cigarette packet and we agreed the deal at £50. I remember her telling me that after a life out in the mission field, she now believed that she was doing her most worthwhile work, in conjunction with embroidery, that of Prayer.

I also wanted to set up a school for prayer back in Shottery parish and had written to Reverend Mother to ask if she would release one or two sisters who might come over to Shottery to help. The responses had been encouraging and so I booked myself in to go over to Malvern Link and be admitted to the Presence. I was greeted by the Prioress and we walked along yards and yards of dimly lit passages and past myriads of statues of saints until the Prioress knocked at a door and I was ushered in. Well, I did not know where to put myself, let alone what to say. Most of us would have a fairly traditional perception of a Reverend Mother. Need I say more? Well this one was just not like that. She was young and she was very attractive. She smiled at my more than obvious acute embarrassment but then quickly endeavoured to put my mind at rest and settle down to the business of the day.

The Holy Rood Sisters at Thirsk were a favourite visit. We used to go there from Newton Aycliffe and just crash out. The tradition was that as I was Vicar, I treated my colleagues to lunch, there was a delightful Trust House Coaching Inn in the market square, so we decided to go there. Somehow or other Reverend Mother found out and I was taken aside with the remark that, "Father, I understand you have made alternative arrangements for lunch." But they were good. If you needed a sister to talk to, there would be one just around the corner and if you needed peace and quiet then there would be no sisters anywhere to be seen, they had amazing sensitivity. It was a great shame when they made a corporate decision to be released from their vows and go back into Civvy Street. I know that a decision like that would not have been made lightly, but I continue to remember them with much affection. In the early days they brought the Gospel message into the back streets of Middlesbrough in the vicinity of the docks. If you have been around there and dipped into the history books you will discover what mission really is like. Somewhat different to what it is perceived to be down in the Home Counties.

I also had some connections with the Sisters of St. Denys at Warminster. One of them came from Stratford upon Avon and had been a Sunday school teacher at Holy Trinity, but when she came back on leave to see her family, she always worshipped with me.

There was a confirmation one Sunday and she came along to support us, but so did another nun: I believe her to have been a member of the Holy Paraclete Sisters from Whitby, but I did not get chance to talk to her. What I did find out though, was that she had walked down Church Lane and (much to the chagrin of the Roman Catholics who were outside their church), this nun walked past and entered the Anglican Church down the road. I did get to stay with the sisters on one occasion and that was when I had gone to an Induction in the town. I cannot remember much other than it was the time of that incredible Test match, known to this day as Botham's Test when very unexpectedly, England won.

I have made brief visits to the Poor Clare's at Freeland and also the Sisters of St. John the Baptist at Alum Rock Road in Birmingham. Then there was a fleeting visit to what was left of the Holy Family Sisters at St. Leonard's on Sea and the All Hallows Sisters at Ditchingham in Norfolk. They seem to be very lively with plenty of plant and buildings which they put to use for conferences and parish training days etc.

The other two orders which I particularly remember are the Benedictines at West Malling where the Mass starts off with the non religious and the religious kept very separate until you get to the peace when we all gather around the main altar which is central to a magnificent concrete chapel, part of, and adjoining an 11th century abbey. Reverend Mother was very tiny, but she exuded a spiritual authority which was clear for all to see and experience. As is often the case in these places, there was not much doubt as to who was boss. One thing stood out here and that was an Anglican Cistercian priest celebrating mass off the cuff! Amazing!

The Benedictines of Burford (at the time) were an interesting group, being an off shoot of the Wantage Sisters. A gorgeous old building and a prayerful tradition going back three centuries that one day there would be a Religious Community there. Somewhat old fashioned but the food was fabulous, which compensated for an odd Eucharistic rite. I made the fateful decision to leave early after my retreat, thus avoiding Reverend Mother, but I was too slow and I was summoned to the presence to make my formal farewells.

The Holy Cross Sisters have now taken on the full Benedictine Mantle and sign themselves OSB. They have certainly been around, in the old days they ran a Convent School down south, and then they moved to Rempstone which is near to Loughborough. I had my own personal and private oratory, so felt myself to have been afforded full spiritual goodies. Reverend Mother was charming and I sat with her at the top table under a very fearsome painting of Reverend Mother Foundress, while we were "entertained" to readings about the martyrologies of selected saints. Perhaps this is not what you might have thought of as being an accompaniment to lunch? But that is how they do things in convents.

Chapter 6

CIVIC MINISTRY

On the face of it, the above form of ministry is to be avoided at all costs; well, that is what I had thought for many years! To my mind, it was the old story of the Church of England being wheeled out each year to say nice things to nice people and it was terribly British and nobody was upset. As far as what was being said in the pulpit, it was invariably tending towards the liberal agenda and generally could be relied upon not to offend. There would be a drinks party afterwards and everyone would have gone home and studiously avoided any church the following Sunday. So what was the point?

Well, it is a matter of expectations really. When I arrived at Alcester, I had not much experience of such matters other than some really big Royal British Legion events up north. Down here, I found that I had to cope with the Court Leet. Fortunately, I had done some research and established that such bodies are now just vestiges of a past glory. There were some who still felt that the Court Leet had a legal role to play, but quite honestly that all went out with Local Government reorganisation in the 70s. Having said that, I know for a fact that our American Cousins would readily die for this sort of thing.

A Court Leet is the Baronial Court of the Lord of the Manor. It is the old form of local government in the good old days when everyone knew their place in society. A High Bailiff was appointed who headed up a body of individuals who kept law and order and maintained certain standards in the matter of food and drink. Nowadays it is purely charitable in its intentions and raises substantial sums of money for worthy causes.

Yet, there was still an expectation that there should be an annual service in church towards which all the local worthies made their annual pilgrimage. I took one look at the order of service from previous years and was horrified. It was a liturgical nightmare and drastic pruning was needed which I dealt with as a priority. The other problem of course was that of where people sat. We still have this problem, but thank goodness it is not as troublesome as it once was. There was an instant clash of swords because I was told that it was the custom for men to sit on one side and for women to sit on the other. I remember saying that I did not know where this tradition had stemmed from and we were certainly not in a Synagogue. I explained that there was a different tradition in the church!

The entire Court Leet paraded up the High Street, accompanied by the town band and other civic dignitaries from the various councils. You could tell by looking at the faces of the visiting councillors that they were wondering what they had let themselves in for. It was exactly the same in reverse when the service had finished, other than the Court Leet paraded in front of the ladies of the various members. There was then a sumptuous repast in the Town Hall when the health of the Lord of the Manor was drunk and the meeting was concluded with a call not to consort with serving wenches who might be around. Basically this just meant that everyone moved on to the Holly Bush Hotel next door.

The Royal British Legion was a different kettle of fish, the big problem was that we had just recovered from the Court Leet festivities in mid October and it was then time for Remembrance Sunday. However, Remembrance Sunday was just that little bit special, the Lord of the Manor, Hugh, 8th Marquess of Hertford had served with the Grenadier Guards and so he led the Legion Guard up the High Street with brolly and bowler, of course. It was quite a sight and attracted visitors from neighbouring communities.

Over the years this parade just grew and grew until close on 1000 persons would be gathered outside the church and focussed on the war memorial. After the traditional ceremonies, it was then a question of who got into church first. I have ended up, perched on the altar or squeezed into some corner. It was just a case of packing people in as best as we could. Most knew that I would not be hanging around and that they would be marching back to the Town Hall before mid-day, having been out by the cenotaph and also in church. The important thing was to make this occasion relevant to the young people, and I was especially pleased with this attitude. After my first big parade in Alcester, one of the old soldiers came up to me to thank me, saying that I had got it right, with not too much glory. I wonder if politicians would have any views on that.

In later years it was clear that many Alcester folk who had come up to the High Street would like to hang around for a while even if they could not get into church. Needless to say there was nothing for them to do and nowhere to go. Not a glimmer of a coffee shop. Fortunately, it did not take long for enterprising retailers to appreciate that there was ready- made business which does now mean that it has become a definite community event.

There was clearly going to be an ecumenical dimension to this sort of thing and I remember telling the other churches that I would never want to put them through a Court Leet Service but would value their attendance on Remembrance Sunday. We all stood outside for the preliminaries and then it was a question of who wanted to join us inside. I did make the point that on this occasion it was the big day for the old soldiers, so as far as I was concerned, they sat at the front. There was always a first rate Sunday roast lunch in the Town Hall to warm us all up and hot soup was served out to the youngsters who had paraded. All in all a first rate occasion which did a lot to foster good links between different factions of the community. However the Court Leet and Royal British Legion were a good start but there were other opportunities for civic ministry at all levels, starting with the Town Council who were persuaded to come to Church for an Annual Service.

I used to enjoy these occasions because I had been a Local Government Councillor many years ago: returned unopposed as an Independent on Old Milverton Parish Council. I enjoyed the work and met some interesting people. I even met up with those who I had played rugby against in the dim and distant past. At this sort of level, I am more than happy. Councillors come into local government because they have a sense of duty and public service. The problems start further up the line at the higher levels of power!

When there was a civic service, I determined that I would be inviting the council to join my local congregation for their normal Sunday service. There were a few mutters, mostly expressing concern that as it was a Parish Eucharist, that would preclude some people from taking a full part, either because they came from another christian communion or as it was most likely, because they did not go to church. As far as other christians were concerned, I had no problems with intercommunion on these special occasions, people needed to examine their own consciences; and as for the others, they just needed to decide if they actually wanted to come to church. I need not have worried. Many of those who did not normally grace the door of any church actually enjoyed the experience and practising christians were delighted that it was a Parish Eucharist and that they were going to receive communion. It was quite instructive to see that the political echelons are well and truly permeated by christianity and they are more than happy to cross any perceived political divide in matters of morals and ethics. Hope for us all yet!

I think that what really changed my mind about civic services was after one of these said services which had gone off well, and was being topped off by good quality refreshments in the Town Hall. I got into conversation with one of the councillors from further north in the county. She was a Tory and devout christian and expressed her concern to me about the state of health of her Labour opponent on her local council who was also a devout christian. She clearly had a lot of time for him and begged me to hold him up in my prayers, which I readily agreed to do. I began to think that even Politicians had souls!

Then we had a service for the Chairman of the District Council. Eric was Captain of the Bell Tower and also a member of our choir. Only he could sing the "Kyrie" which meant a bit of shuffling around in the front seat, but we managed and as I had cunningly suggested that we go one stage further and turn the service in to a Solemn Eucharist (with incense), this meant a little bit of variety which actually went down quite well. There were some Roman Catholics around who chuckled at the experience, after all their own church had basically got rid of incense some years previously. And for those who thought that incense was just not the thing to do, then I had a ready reply. It was only used for very special occasions!

The next time that I had a big civic service experience was in Coventry Cathedral when I preached at the memorial service for the four fire-fighters who had died in the tragedy at Atherstone on Stour. I did not have much control about that, but I need not have worried because there was a first rate Precentor who was not going to be pushed around by politicians or anyone else. I just sat back and let him get on with it. It was the only time that I have heard a priest of the Church of England actually say, "In my professional judgement, this needs to be done and therefore we will do it". Good on him and perhaps a few more of those in authority might be moved to take the same line. One thing that civic services have taught me is that you need to prepare, to prepare well and if necessary you need to have some rehearsals so that when it comes to the crunch, people actually know what they are supposed to be doing. I generally find that that is what they want.

Civic duties can cover other social areas as well. Starting off a meeting for example or actually just being there. I am very much a supporter of "being" because I reckon that is what it is all about. Not saying, not doing, but being! As many will know, I am a keen exponent of the game with the oval shaped ball. Rugby clubs are very keen that any formal dinner should always start with a grace – of sorts! It is a good way to instil some "hush" into the proceedings and gives the evening a good start. I was absolutely delighted at one particular Shottery RFC dinner to find that our guest speaker, the legendary J.P.R. Williams of immortal fame was not just a practising christian but also a churchwarden and he most certainly expected a grace! I must confess though, that I have made up some appropriate graces that have fitted in with the occasion and that they have been of a rustic nature.

You also get the "one offs" and there is no way that you can prepare for them. It is really a question of prayer and letting your training take over to cover a multitude of sins. The wedding of the Earl of Yarmouth in my first few months ended up by being fairly straightforward. This was in part due to the very convenient fact that not many civic dignitaries had been invited; it was just the staff at Ragley and a fair proportion of the aristocracy from this country and from abroad. It could not have been easier. It was just a question of the traditional arrangements for any wedding and making sure that everyone knew what they were doing. It went like a charm.

There was another event which involved Ragley and was of a very pleasant nature. This was the dedication of a delightful new stained glass window in church in memory of John Emrys Jones, one of my predecessors. Bishop Simon came to do the necessary, but had declined my invitation to Sunday lunch beforehand. What I did not know was that the marquess and the bishop were at school together and wanted to catch up on past times. Now there was every sort of civic dignitary present that you could think of and they were late and there had been no phone call to explain. I subsequently discovered that there had been a car crash outside the Ragley gate and this had rather screwed things up. Bishop Simon could always be guaranteed to arrive at least 30 minutes before any event, so I knew that we had problems. In the end, it all went very well and it was a good opportunity to have a quiet word with the politicians about one or two matters that had aroused my concern in the Alcester area.

I must admit that despite my cynicism, there are definite advantages in these services or events; the church gets access and time, also the opportunity to quietly fix one or two problems anonymously. I think it has been said of some of the top diplomats in the world that their greatest achievements are never known because a quiet word with someone can ensure that the potential heat of a conflict can be removed at a stroke and nothing gets in the papers. It is the same with the Church and we come back to my basic premise that in priestly ministry, you need to get involved and make sure that you are known. It pays handsome dividends on all fronts. So at the end of the day, experience has taught me, that on this matter, I needed to change my views.

Above: A big surprise on the Severn Valley.
Below: On board the "Ivatt".

Above: Storming through Highley.
Below: With the Alcester Court Leet.

Above: Wayside with Peter and Stephen.
Below: "Tornado" on the West Somerset Railway.

Above: Woody Bay Station, Lynton & Barnstaple Railway.
Below: Son Mark, and grandsons Joel and Nathan see off the last train.

Above: My favourite locomotive "King George V" at Swindon.
Below: High Mass Epiphany, 2013.

Taking a break on a "Prairie".

Above: The Boss, Rowan Williams, pops in for a drink.
Below: The Boss with my first book "The Fiery Canon" with Hilary looking on.

My final procession.

Chapter 7

MUSIC

Music has played a big part in my life, especially as a priest. When I was a youngster in Woodstock, I received the inevitable piano lessons and by the time we left to go to north Warwickshire, I had passed Grade V with distinction. In Rugby, I managed to get in on an organ scholarship which gave me basically one year free of charge on the parish church organ with a local teacher. When I arrived at Rugby School, I found that the standard was amazingly high, in fact there were at least five full time music teachers employed by the school. I remember telling my piano teacher that I would like to try my hand at the Grieg Piano Concerto. I was told that it was too easy and promptly given some obscure piece by the Danish composer, Neilsen. I always regretted that I did not put my foot down on that one. But there was always the organ and there were three of them at Rugby, although I was banned from the chapel four manual version and had to content myself with the two manual in the memorial chapel and the three manual in the Temple Speech Room, which admittedly could make a decent noise.

Rugby was very keen on House music competitions and I was soon dragged into that scenario. Town House had a particularly good reputation and always got to the finals. I accompanied a clarinettist on the piano, but unfortunately the visiting judge did not like my interpretation which incidentally had been agreed with all and sundry. I was marked down and we lost. The next year, I was told that I could keep my place in the first team but would have to content myself with tapping a milk bottle in an obscure piece by Bartok. That did not suit so I dropped down to the second team and had a wonderful experience. It was decided that we play a trio by Smetana. It was quite long, 20 minutes in fact, but just great fun and to add to the occasion we insisted on three grand pianos, which after much muttering from the porters, we eventually gained. I have to say that we brought the house down and won by a big margin. I still have the music score to this day.

It was some time though before I returned to music and the opportunity came when I started at Wells Theological College. There was a free residential course at the Royal School of Church Music, so I signed up and it gave me the chance to work with those who in years to come would be the organists and choirmasters of our big cathedrals. It was a wonderful course and gave me the opportunity to hone my singing skills. Then I realised that there was to be a plainsong class and so I slipped in to sit at the feet of the best plainsong teachers in England. Later that week we sang plainsong evensong in Croydon parish church and I certainly raised my game just by being in the company of all those top musicians. Back to Wells, where we had lessons from the previous cathedral organist in chanting the versicles and responses, plus the eucharistic canon and soon I was feeling very confident. In addition, I was able to sign up for discounted lessons on the cathedral organ itself from the resident organist. What a treat! What a mighty instrument! I was also college sacristan and so early in the morning I would let myself into a medieval cathedral to lay up for the college eucharist and then slip up the organ steps and have a few minutes before the college arrived for their early devotions. When you pull out the stops and give it the full treatment, the cathedral shakes.

Every Friday night the college finished up the week by singing plainsong compline in the fourteenth century chapel which was at the top of Vicars Close. I was soon signed up for the singing/chanting team and it was just a delightful occasion all round. Once the move to Salisbury was completed I was able to try my hand at canting in the magnificat at evensong in the cathedral. That was also a wonderful occasion and the following week, I covered the entire service which was most gratifying. Cathedral evensong may not be everyone's cup of tea, but it has its advantages and meant that when various liturgical and musical sundries cropped up in parish life, I was able to cope.

I well remember the night before the birth of Stephen. It was Maundy Thursday in County Durham and I had got a priest in to cover for me at the Maundy Thursday mass with all the liturgical trimmings. The one problem was that he could not sing, so I recorded myself singing the whole of Psalm 22 in plainsong which was duly played during the washing of the feet. As so often happens on these occasions, Stephen came a bit late, on Good Friday actually. Still it was a joy to see my new born son in Church for the Easter Morning Eucharist and I was able to sing the exultet with great gusto.

The exultet is an ancient prayer/canticle which relates to the idea of light coming into the darkness and assisting us to see everything. It is sung towards the beginning of the Paschal Mass on Holy Saturday night and traditionally is sung by the Deacon. What I used to do was to wear my priests stole in the deacon position and do the singing myself. For some odd reason, I could always guarantee that I would have a cough at this important time, so a glass of water was always balanced on the pulpit.

Alcester was a very musical place with plenty of professional musicians. My first organist was well qualified and went on to be ordained. Richard had that great ability to get the best out of people, even if the material was far from promising. At the same time, I found to my joy that my PCC secretary was an opera singer and so for a few years we were treated to the famous Easter Hymn from Cavalleria Rusticana and on Ash Wednesday to the Agnus Dei from The Mozart Requiem. An absolute luxury and I just sat back and soaked it up.

It did not take long before I had to accept the fact that my singing days were over. I had become gravelly and it was better just to say the mass rather than spoil it with roughly sung interspersions. There is nothing worse than going to some of these Anglo-catholic churches, where to sing the entire mass is *de rigeur* irrespective as to the quality of the singing. I totally disagree. At the end of the day, for whose glory are we celebrating the Eucharist? It should be worthy. Much better to keep it simple and understandable. One can always get a professional in for the very big occasions. A parish priest cannot be good at everything; he should have the humility to bring in a specialist from time to time if necessary. Our GPs do not seem to have a problem on that score.

Now, the actual worship or liturgy, to my mind falls quite naturally as a partner to music. I enjoy taking services, which is perhaps why liturgy was really my best subject at college. Liturgy means the work of the people and emphasises the very definite contribution from the laity. At the end of the day, having offered praise and Glory to God, it is important that the laity are given the opportunity to partake, because the last thing we want is a priest ridden church. I can think of nothing worse.

The beauty about the study of liturgy is its breadth. It encompasses the scriptures, doctrine and church history in varying degrees. The act of worship is the response of the community of Faith to God. It can be repentant, praising, adoring, supplicating, but it is a response and needs to be positive. When I was at Wells, we were told that all services started on time, to the second, or the cathedral bell, after all, one had an appointment with the Almighty and God help you if you had the temerity to be late. It was on occasions like that when apparently sleepy and bemused elderly clergy could get quite agitated; in other words the college lecturing staff came into their own and then, apparently went back to sleep again. We all knew that was not the case and there were very few delays in starting. But once you got started, there was no guarantee that you would be allowed to proceed without interruptions. The wrong pronunciation of a word from the bible, pausing when you should not etc, would bring a sharp response. At the end of the day, this was the place to get it right, because in church it would be too late. On more than one occasion the remark was made that the college had a responsibility to the poor unsuspecting public. Fair comment. Badly taken worship is an insult to God.

I was brought up on the "Shape of the Liturgy" by Dom Gregory Dix who was an Anglican Benedictine from the Nashdom Community. It was rumoured that even Rome would make contact with him for advice, so he must have been good. I have a copy of his book which was given to me by the late Bishop John Daly and it has pride of place on my bookshelf. To my mind the structure of the mass is all important and it is fascinating to see how it has developed over the years from the basic words of institution by Our Lord at the last Supper.

One of my lecturers had completed his doctoral thesis purely on these words of institution. I have a copy and thoroughly enjoyed reading it, mind you we used to enjoy getting him off the subject at lectures; it transpired that he also had a degree in Mechanical Engineering and knew how to take a steam engine to pieces and also how to put it back together again. It should not surprise anyone to learn that he was a big supporter of the Ffestiniog Railway and ended up as President. We clergy get in on all sorts of things don't we?

But to return to the altar. There are all sorts of names for the service par excellence and which is a sure guarantee of the imparting of grace and you can choose from mass, eucharist, liturgy, holy communion, breaking of bread, to name but a few. The problem with the Church of England has been the vast array of orders of service.

Now is not the time to look at the early Anglican prayer books in detail. Much could be said about the liturgy of the 1549 version, (greatly loved by

Michael Ramsey), followed by the much more Protestant based 1552 book. A slight amendment in 1559 and then the glories of the 1662 prayer book landed on the lecterns of all parish churches throughout the land and for the next 300 years, there was no canonical alternative. All priests of the Church of England are required to declare their agreement at their Institution to a living and assistant curates receive similar treatment at their ordination. So there was no getting away from it and this has left the church with a big problem, because when eventually the liturgical log jam was cleared, all sorts of genies popped out of the liturgical bottle and we have been living with that one ever since. There were attempts by the Anglo-Catholic wing to introduce some changes with a 1928 prayer book, but it was deemed to be too "High" and was thrown out. It made no difference however, because the Anglo-Catholics just used it anyway. So much for canonical obedience!

In my time I have used 1662, 1928 mea culpa, interim rite, Series 1, Series 2, Series 3, Rite A and Common Worship with all its alternatives. Dare I confess that on one or two visits to Anglo Catholic churches to help out with sickness or holiday cover I have had to cope with the Roman Rite. I must say that I do not like it at all. I can find all the Catholicity that I require in the Anglican rites.

I am a great believer in not just starting on time, but actually starting as if you are in control and know what you want. At the end of the day, people wish to be guided through the rite and you are the trained leader with the authority to do so. I am a great believer in using silence at suitable points and leadership requires that you control those who just want to keep going at all costs. Liturgy needs sensitive handling; you need to feel your way through the service.

When it comes to the mass, it is worth remembering that we are talking about a drama. It is a dramatic calling to mind of the one great saving act of redemption all those years ago. This is why I look upon the celebrating priest as being "Alter Christus" so that in the calling to mind of those wonderful acts of redemption, we are actually there, in on the act and very present at this powerful occasion. A look at the Jewish Passover celebrations will show the closeness of the two rites and this approach of feeling that you are very much present. The rite brings the past into the present and then projects it into the future.

I also like to wear what I perceive to be appropriate vesture, in other words a chasuble. I like the historical context, as it is the shape of the shawls that the shepherds of Galilee wear to this day and of course it has been worn by priests of the more Catholic persuasion for centuries. But the most important thing about wearing the chasuble is that it removes the personality of the priest. It is not Fr. Smith at the altar, but a representative of Our Lord. Priesthood is about humility even for the most outward going of priests, we might dress up, so to speak, but there is a purpose in doing so. On the other hand a degree of sensitivity will dictate that there are some occasions when a more simplified approach would be appropriate, such as an outdoor eucharist on the beach or in the woods!

Music and liturgy have a great reputation in the Church of England and throughout the world. When I was on the course at Addington Palace with the Royal School of Church Music, I discovered that one of the students was a Roman Catholic priest. He had been sent by his Bishop to attend the entire three year course and then go back to his diocese and raise the standard of music. Interestingly the Bishop was a former Anglican priest. When Pope Benedict XVI came to this country, he was clearly much moved by the quality of the singing at the choral evensong which had been arranged for him in Westminster Abbey, there was even an Anthem in praise of Our Lady! So good, that the choir was invited over to Rome to sing in the Sistine Chapel where they greatly distinguished themselves. There are Roman Catholic priests in this country who are looking forward to the day when they themselves will be able to preside at a Solemn Choral Evensong. I hope they do not have too long to wait.

I have always been amazed by the devotion of choirs to their church. It is by being a Junior choir master at Lillington Church in the 60s that I eventually discovered my vocation. I put a lot into that position and received much in return, even if the language of choirboys in a football match was rather on the fruity side. There was also the occasion when I lost a choirboy at London Airport on an organised outing, however the vicar seemed totally unconcerned and assured me that the errant choirboy would turn up, which thankfully he did.

There have been times when I have been totally aghast at choir practices and also at services, such as the time when the choirmaster was conducting an anthem in front of the entrance to the choir area and was actually blocking said entrance. The sidesmen came up with the collection and they just lifted him out of the way as he had shown no inclination to move himself. On another occasion there was virtually war declared between the basses and the tenors and yet, at the end of the day, these guys stick around and are incredibly loyal. Yes, it's their life and they would be lost without it, and also to the suggestion that they might like to retire early because their voice is no longer up to it, who is going to tell them? I have chickened out of that one and I don't mind admitting to it.

Those in the Church of England who enjoy criticising should come and attend ordinary parish church worship. It is a totally different world to that of cathedrals. There are most certainly some very awkward people in the pews, you could even advance to the suggestion that they are totally lacking in any Christian principles at all, but they are there in the pews and you have to deal with them. That is the reality of parish life and quite honestly I do not think that many people at the top really understand that.

So, as far as music and liturgy is concerned, I think it is high time that I moved on to reflect on other aspects of the life of the good old Church of England, but to which direction should I turn my attention? I reckon it is that of appointments. Not to Bishoprics as I defer to apparently superior knowledge, but it is to the appointment process as befits the humble parish priest who at the end of the day has given up much to serve his fellow men and women.

Chapter 8

APPOINTMENTS

I have long felt that there is something inherently wrong with the way that the Church of England appoints priests to parishes and bishops to dioceses. To begin with there are too many people involved in the process and some judicious pruning is required. I am all for consultation, but there are limits. The Church of England is supposed to be an episcopal church but is behaving more and more like a congregational church. There are some who feel that anglicanism will provide a suitable syncretism of the opposing modes of ecclesiastical government, but I believe that they are so wide apart that we might as well accept the fact and try to work with what we have.

Needless to say there have been some brilliant appointments and nobody would wish to dispute the fact that the will of God was duly discerned and acted upon. However, there have been some positive disasters and the dioceses have probably ten years to cope until they can have another go. But even if the choice is not exactly to everyone's taste, at least you expect your Bishop to be around. You then find that he or she is expected to pop down to the House of Lords and sit in serried ranks with other bishops of the established church and try to kid everyone that we are a christian country. There are weighty debates and everyone gets terribly excited, but quite honestly, does anyone really care? I would much rather that the Bishops came back to their dioceses to live amongst and minister to their clergy. At the end of the day, the bishop is my parish priest! I remember talking to Hugh, 8th Marquess of Hertford about this very matter and it was quite clear that he was more than happy to wade in and speak on matters of interest to Christians. There has been much talk about ministry of the laity, so here would be a golden opportunity in the House of Lords, but I would readily admit that since the death of Hugh, there have been changes and this would not be so easy.

Why not a straw poll of the clergy? After all, we have more than a passing interest in the matter, in fact, we should hold the majority voting rights – but that will just not happen. Then to add insult to injury, when the appointment is eventually announced and we come to the enthronement, you have to look very hard to see where the clergy are seated in the cathedral. As I suppose it is virtually bound to happen in the established Church, the front seats are taken up by the establishment and the clergy have to be shovelled in to any spare places that are available. This has always annoyed me. The clergy are not asking for much, but on this special day, when their parish priest is formally put in post, it is surely not asking too much for their presence to be acknowledged in a slightly more advantageous manner. Possibly closer in and so feeling very part of the ceremony, rather than as an appendage which had to be accommodated. Still, there have been some interesting variations. I believe that a previous Bishop of Bristol arrived at Temple Meads Station from Swindon in a High Speed Train with half of his congregation and for which he received a 50% discount. I am sure that more pastoral approaches have been used in the countryside. Back to parishes.

I want to start with a true story. There is a parish priest in the midlands who has served in his parish for a very long time. He is single and was basically sent there for his first incumbency because nobody else was interested. It is not the most beautiful of parishes, in fact is downright boring and featureless but over 20,000 people live there and they all have souls. It was a hard ministry with precious few material rewards, but our priest gamely soldiered on until one day he was asked by a fellow priest why he had not moved? After all, he had done his innings so to speak and kept his nose clean. The answer was quite simple. Our friend had not moved because his bishop had not asked him to move. He was completely at the disposal of his bishop! Sounds a bit old fashioned doesn't it? But there are still priests around like him. Not for them, the sylvan pastures of Barchester, but for them there are at least the basic satisfactions that they have been true to their vocation and their rewards are to come. I cannot see many priests in the more comfortable areas even considering such a possibility. Much talk, but precious little walk!

It may surprise readers to know that when I was in County Durham, one of my curates came to ask permission to be absent from the parish for one night so that he could go and support his mother while his father was actually dying. The reason for this was that Fr. Frank had been a member of the Company of Mission Priests. These priests will work as a small chapter of perhaps three priests in a very rough parish. They are all celibate and live in the parsonage. There is a senior priest, who is the incumbent, but his stipend goes into the central pot and this is enough to feed three priests, house them and keep them warm. They are still around today and are another unsung example of priests in the Church of England being at the total disposal of the authorities.

It therefore irritates me when I see the processes that are in place today for the appointment of an incumbent and it confirms what other people have said, and that is that some parishes just do not deserve to have a priest. You can preach until the cows come home about stewardship, you can gently set the scene so that all can see the true costs involved, but I am afraid you are wasting your time. When it comes down to it, they want a priest on their terms and one who will carry on just as they have done so for many years before. They will want a full representation on the appointing committee so that they can ensure they get their cut, irrespective of the needs of others. Often it will be the most assertive persons in the parish with a complete lack of sensitivity and ability to make a valid judgement. Whereas there will be someone from a parish who may be very quiet, but who has the superb ability to discern. It seems to me that if we are going to go down this line, and I am not convinced that we should be so doing, then we need to ensure a consistently high standard of interviewers. How we do that, is another matter. Perhaps we should go back to well and trusted methods of the past, when the bishop really did want to ascertain the views of the parish, but at the end of the day, he made the appointment, after all he was the bishop. The problem today is that of money, or to be more accurate, lack of money. If such monies have to come from the pockets or purses of parishioners, then they are going to want some say. How do we do it?

I hate the idea of any form of political interference, but the church may have to go down that line at first so that it can map out a strategy that is fit for purpose. The problem is that there are not many votes in sorting out the problems of the established church, especially if they are self inflicted. There would be more votes in sorting out the prisons! But, I am sure it could still be done. If there is a will then there will be a way! Efficiency is a term beloved by politicians and that would need a desire to restrict drastically the number of PCCs so that the authorities would not have to go through the expense of dealing with tiny little PCCs with tiny congregations. These PCCs must though be truly representative of the smaller villages which by definition would need to be incorporated within them. Possibly an agreed quota of representatives, but ensuring that at the end of the day, the main centre of ministry would have the voting power to ensure that progress was made. I know it is easier said than done, but it must be tried. Then there would be the possibility of abolishing deaneries which in most cases are just talking shops, and concentrate on large parish/ministry groupings with a possible rejuvenation of archdeaconries. I hate to say it, but in both financial and administrative terms, small is no longer beautiful.

So, we have a vacancy in a parish. How long should the interregnum last? The dioceses differ on this one. Perhaps someone on high could possibly inform the parishes of the legal position? I certainly know of one diocese that takes a most refreshing line on this particular matter and will not be bound by dates and time lags. It would appear that bishops and patrons can just get on with it. I have to confess that I prefer the old method. Once a benefice becomes vacant, there would be a short gap so that everyone could recover their breath and the former incumbent be given the time to make a dignified exit. I have always said that there should be time for the parish to get the old incumbent out of its hair – but not too long!

Then I would hope that the bishop would make contact with the parish and arrange for the wardens to meet up with him and that they bring proposals with them as to the sort of priest they feel that the parish needs at this point in time. I would also hope that the Rural Dean would be consulted at an early stage. Then the Bishop would meet with his council and there would be prayer and the process of discernment before a name could be suggested. To my mind, this is what a Bishop should be doing. Rather than hordes of glossy advertisements decorating the inside covers of the Church Times and giving the false impression that everything is all singing and all dancing, it is the time for discerning episcopal direction. The parish representatives then need to meet up with the proposed incumbent and see if they are in full agreement. I would hope that there would be sufficient trust in a diocese to ensure that this would be the likely scenario. The bishops would consult their own lists and also a type of clearing house and the parish would have to right to ask for a second look and if all else fails, rejection, but that would have to be very much the exception to the rule.

However, the good old Church of England has decided that a more congregational approach is required and that there must be total clarity. I would not mind so much, if the authorities could just get on with it, but deep down I detect the need to be seen to be on a par with the secular world and to be seen to be "with it". Never mind about prayer and discernment, never mind about God's will, as long as we are seen to be jogging along with the world, then all will be well. But do we have to be seen to be always going along a well trodden path? There is at least one other well trodden path and that is the path of righteousness, because it is the path of Jesus. I well remember an appointment in this diocese when the wardens took a very aggressive attitude with the bishop and archdeacons. It was basically, we know best and you will just have to agree with what we want because we have the money and will withdraw it if you get in our way. Now, although the church needs to appreciate the world that surrounds it, it is surely entitled to both reflect and pray about these appointments. I am not so sure that lengthy parish profiles are the way forward, especially if they have to be drawn up only in one particular way to satisfy current thinking. Parish priests should be given training on how to draw up their own CV which can then be circulated to appropriate bishops and patronage boards. I just feel that there should be more time given to the clergy especially when they come towards the end of their training period. Priest and parish need to fit together and a bad appointment can be absolutely disastrous.

In an interview situation, there is a really dangerous possibility of everything being put onto the interview, to the detriment of other factors. There are many, clergy included, who can talk the hind leg off a donkey and in so doing, they can impress those who they think need to be impressed and not necessarily the correct people. I have always thought that if parishes and bishops want to go down this line there needs to be some agreement as to what proportions should be ascribed to interview, attitude, completed application form etc. I know that some parishes request that a short sermon be preached. I fully accept that it is not easy and mistakes made can lead to a lot of unhappiness later on. There are of course children and schools to be considered and any possible reasonable additional requirements. At the end of the day, this is not any normal job and the incumbent will be putting in many hours in his or her service to the parish. The whole idea of a stipend is to relieve the incumbent from the worry of earning enough money to buy food etc and to heat the parsonage. We are not talking about luxuries, but adequacies and that should extend to the working expenses as well.

I know that what I have elucidated is not going to be taken up, but I do admit to feeling rather better for having got it off my chest. But when the choice is about to be made, it is imperative that the dioceses inform the applicants of any undercurrents that they are aware of. I have heard of too many occasions when problem parishes were dressed up to be miracle parishes and it has been a downright lie. There is no need for that.

Chapter 9

MISCELLANEOUS LITURGICAL FACTORS

I thought it might be opportune to clarify some of the more distant services or artefacts that are used in the church and which in some places are viewed with extreme suspicion. I imagine that the use of incense has caused more liturgical aggro than anything else. Perhaps I might help to try and clarify what it is all about.

I suspect that some people are still living at the time of the Reformation and have a "thing" about incense, while other people just do not like it, often for medical reasons.

I remember being frowned at when I just happened to mention that I would be using it at a special occasion; I would add that to my mind it should only be used at special occasions. This would include the main eucharist of the week, funeral requiems and weddings. The frowning parishioner felt that to use incense was too much like the Roman Catholic Church. Well, this played straight into my trap as I was able to explain that the use of incense was virtually a guarantee that the service would be in accordance with the rites of the Church of England! At that time the Roman Catholics had all but got rid of incense.

Incense is the dry ground powder from a gum resin found in Arabia and has been used for centuries by other religious faiths in their acts of prayer and worship. When we talk about incense in the church we are talking about God and therefore about divinity. You may well recall in the New Testament that during Roman control it was sometimes decreed that all people should worship the Emperor, who from time to time determined to take to himself, divine status. You were expected to offer incense in front of an available statue to the divine Emperor and then that showed your loyalty. Needless to say, the christians refused and immediately were marked down for severe punishment.

Today in the church it is burned by sprinkling it on glowing charcoal cubes which have been specially lit in a container which is called a thurible.

A prayer of blessing is offered and the thurible is set so that it can be swung so as to give full effect to the burning incense. It is all about the divinity of Jesus and so it helps to set the scene at the beginning of the service and also to emphasize that Jesus is always present in our liturgical celebrations which are to follow; in addition, there is a sense of cleansing.

In any procession, it is always the incense which comes first, followed by the cross; God in Christ comes first. The high altar is censed before we start, followed by the censing of the gospels, because it is not just in sacrament, but also in word, that God in Christ is coming to us. It is important and the incense helps to be a testament to that fact. Finally, when the altar has been prepared and the gifts of the people have been offered, then everything on the altar is censed and set aside for a very special purpose.

There are other times that the incense is offered, such as when the sacrament is raised at the altar and also at services such as benediction, together with special processions. It is serious, but there can be times of humour, especially in Wells Cathedral, when the thurible was being swung perhaps rather more lustily than it should have been, with the result that the bottom bit detached and flew off like a fiery comet.

Now on to the sacrament of penance, reconciliation, also called confession. Many Anglicans shudder when they hear the term confession and again I reckon that many people are still living at the time of the Reformation and really ought to update their religion. The first point to clarify is that all priests in the Church of England are given the authority to grant absolution, which by definition must also include the ability to hear confessions. At the actual laying on of hands at an ordination, the Bishop speaks very special words which give this authority. All you have to do is to turn to the Book of Common Prayer in the service of the visiting of the sick and you will find there in its entirety all that happens at such a time as the hearing of a confession, including the actual words of absolution. Yes this is in the Church of England and it has always been there. You can also look at the early part of the communion rite where there is reference to the quieting of conscience and the ministration of ghostly counsel and advice.

Clearly there is some fear here and the jocular approach of Dave Allen has probably not helped. There has been in the past too much secrecy, too much emphasis on sin and not enough joy in redemption. Confession is about being honest with yourself for a change. In many ways it is like going to see your GP, confidential discussions take place and medicines are prescribed. The seal of the confessional is absolute in the Church of England and following on, spiritual medicines are prescribed. In the Roman Catholic Church there is what is referred to as, "The Box". There is a good point here though, because nobody can touch anybody and that is well known. In the Church of England there is a feeling that there should be better observation and no ideas of anything going on in a shady corner. Normally a prayer desk suffices or even just kneeling at the altar; all you need to ensure is that there is nobody around who is within earshot. Having said that, the seal of the confessional still applies.

When I started at Wells Theological College, in my very first week I was being trained to hear confessions. I well remember the sessions, because the lecturer was the former vicar of the church of the University of Oxford. He, like Newman before him had brought back the sacrament as there was clearly a need for it. We used as a primer a book published by a Methodist minister! The book was called *Five for Sorrow, Ten for Joy*! I recall being told that the Church of England took a slightly more pragmatic approach to the hearing of confessions. All could, some should, but none ought! I learned a lot in those early days and also the ability to laugh which is very important for a confessor.

I have heard quite a few confessions over the years and I always remember what I was taught in those early years, which encompasses humility and sensitivity. To see the joy on the face of someone who has received the mark of absolution is a great privilege and I never forget to ask the penitent to pray for me a sinner also; then we are all on a level playing field. I ran across the road and was nearly knocked down by a bus after my first confession. Joy, joy!

Incense and confessions can be found in abundance at the Shrine of our Lady of Walsingham, and yet this is something that still arouses suspicion in the Church of England. What a shame, because the shrine has many supporters from those groupings which normally would not be seen to be within this particular orbit. I can think of no better examples than those of our two Archbishops, namely, Justin of Canterbury and John of York. Thousands of people go each and every year, mostly Anglicans of course, but there will always be some Roman Catholics who rather like the way that the Church of England does these sorts of things and an increasing number of Christians from the Free Church tradition. To top it off nicely there is even an Orthodox Chapel within the walls of the Anglican shrine, so all traditions can be catered for.

Walsingham is all about the Incarnation and the public ministry of Jesus up and until his death. What is so special to christians about Jesus is that the word became flesh and the divine shared with the human. Majesty shared with poverty and glory shared with humility. The use of incense emphasizes the actuality of divinity within our experience. Jesus is not just man, he is God as well.

When you arrive at Walsingham, you will find a fairly traditional Norfolk village, constructed of flint and other local materials. The Anglican shrine is very much part of the community and without it, the village would be totally lost. The tradition of pilgrimage goes back, close on 1000 years to a time when the lady of the manor had a vision and was required by the Virgin Mary to build a replica of the Holy House of Nazareth. English sovereigns made pilgrimages over the years including the redoubtable Henry VIII, who inevitably felt that he could do with the wealth and cash which had accrued over the years and promptly pulled it down.

Pilgrimages can be made as part of a group or singly, they can last just for one day or much longer; accommodation and food is first rate, you certainly will not starve. Usually, one starts with a visit to the Holy House where prayer is offered and a candle lit, there then might be the opportunity to attend mass or to engage with a full session of Stations of the Cross. This is a biblically based spiritual exercise when you walk around the garden pausing at various, statues/paintings that depict the walk of Our Lord to Calvary.

There are processions around the gardens when either a statue of our lady is carried or the Blessed Sacrament is exposed. Following on from the processions, there are sermons and the opportunity to receive the gift of grace through the healing ministries which are on offer, with Holy Water, Holy Oil or Penance.

There is usually much laughter on a pilgrimage and it is just good fun to be part of a Christian community and away from your own community. It is not a retreat and if you go around looking terribly pious and miserable, then quite honestly, I think you have gone to the wrong place. Many people take the opportunity to visit the seaside for an afternoon and get some fresh air inside of them; again it is also a chance to let your hair down a bit. Why not? For some people this is their only opportunity of getting away and having a break. What better place than Walsingham and the Norfolk Coast?

Chapter 10

MISSION

There has been and there continues to be much talk in the Church of England about mission. Weighty papers are drawn up and then discussed at every possible level of synodical government. Serious academic discussion ensues and ultimately we are all encouraged to follow the path of mission, to keep foreign fields of influence in our prayers and to cough up some money from time to time. The church then returns to some form of fiscal or maintenance discussion which tends to dominate church life. Everyone goes home feeling that they know a bit more about mission and that they continue to live in awe of those who have "gone out there" on our behalf. I am perhaps being a little cynical when I suggest that the most noise about mission made in this country is made by those who really do not know what mission is about. They tend to live in comfortable homes, have been to comfortable schools and have very comfortable incomes. They should get off their backsides and start in this country by living and working in a different area. Go north, I would suggest and see a different world. Then perhaps go abroad. But I digress. Have you a definition of mission? The best one that I heard was from Bishop John Daly, formerly Bishop of Gambia, Gold Coast and finally Korea who said that it was just a question of making friends for Jesus! I like that.

In fairness, there have been some wonderful exponents of mission in our church over the years. Both at home and abroad. Many have died in their missionary pursuits and many have suffered but they still keep going. The really big two missionary bodies which survive have taken on mergers etc, but now seem to be working more together rather than in opposition. We are talking about US (United Society) and CMS (Church Missionary Society). They can be found in most corners of the globe, but are supplemented by other smaller and more specialist missionary bodies. I am a member of both bodies and used to be a governor of Selly Oak College as well as being on Council for USPG as it was in those days. It certainly is very instructive to meet these guys who either come here from abroad for one year or those who are about to go abroad. We have so much to learn from them. In addition they are very gracious and sensitive. You will not feel that you have been lectured.

One thing that I have learned from making these contacts is that you need to understand the importance of local culture. The witness of the Mothers' Union in Ghana for example is very telling. It is big business and the number of members is out of this world and yet women do not take up responsibilities as multifarious as they do in this country. It is easy to criticise, but quite honestly they can show us the way home in many aspects of church life.

As I have alluded, mission is about relationships and in our case it is about relationships with Jesus. I sometimes think that relationships within the church need a healthy stock-take from time to time. Whether it is within the parish, within the diocese or just within the family, there needs to be respect for the human being, for the individual and above all for the opportunity to build up a bond which will hold together and be a witness to others. It was at a missionary conference that I felt the call to go north. I had already signified my willingness to be considered for foreign fields and after a trip down to London, there was even a parish in Zambia that was being considered for me, and then something happened which meant that I did not go and it was all down to an incorrect address in the records of USPG. The formal letter was sent out to me, but it never arrived. There were change-overs of staff and I had got myself involved with the possibilities of going to Durham. It was only some months later that I found out what had really happened, by which time I had accepted the offer of Newton Aycliffe. Only then to find out that if I had waited another two weeks an offer of Burford in the Cotswolds would have been mine. I reckon that somebody else was involved in that one. Any suggestions?

Well, to get back to this conference, it was held at Loughborough University and was entitled *Catholic Renewal 2*. I remember it particularly for the fact that there were hordes of Australians, bishops, priests and laity alike. They were great fun and blocked off access to the bar at night, that was the only black mark that could be ascribed to them. It was interesting to find out that there was a totally different attitude to sabbatical leave out in Australia. It was taken very seriously and you were compelled to take the leave and also, you were generously looked after as far as finance was concerned. How refreshing! In this country, you were usually greeted somewhat grudgingly, especially when it came down to the matter of money. Again there was a lot of talk, but not much action, unless of course you were a diocesan officer and that meant that you had a better chance than us mere parish priests. I should have had five sabbaticals in my time, whereas I only managed to get one. In fairness, this has now improved greatly, but I must admit that I did feel rather aggrieved about it as did other clergy of my ilk.

But we must move on and I must remember that I should practice what I preach. The charge of hypocrisy is a charge that can weigh very heavily unless you clear your brain and your memory. On more than one occasion, I have been preaching and, horror of horrors, I knew what I was about to say could lead to the charge of hypocrisy being levelled at me! Somehow or other, I have been able to talk my way out of it, but there have been close shaves.

Something else may well be of interest and that has been my quest to do some academic reading. It has always been a problem to me that I could never pass exams and it was only the advent of the Open University that enabled me to attain some reasonable level of academic respectability. I am not sure how it happened, but I found myself doing some research about the life and ministry of John Henry, Cardinal Newman. I sat at the feet of his biographer, Fr. Ian Ker and had open access to the Birmingham Oratory. I must confess that I thoroughly enjoyed myself, although I did not always find it easy. However, I developed a very healthy respect for his life and times and to see just how relevant he is even to this day now. As I have already said there is much talk about mission and it is only fair that I might actually offer some suggestions as to how the church or the individual might respond.

I look upon mission as a basic ministry or service which as a christian I am duty bound to both offer and perform. I always look at the story in the gospel of John about the washing of the feet on Maundy Thursday. I view this action as the one great sacramental act that can be acted out for all to witness and be a part of. As it only happens once each year, it is therefore very special. When at college we used to sing a lovely simple, but very moving hymn, entitled *Love is his Word* which I reckon sums it all up. I brought this into my parishes at a later date and everyone thought the choice to be ideal. It was therefore very moving when at my last service, I was able to perform this sacrament while this lovely hymn was being sung.

So, what is the message of Maundy Thursday? It is an extension of the incarnation, that other great miracle, whereby we are bidden to get involved with the world, because Jesus clearly got involved with us. It is a question of rolling up your sleeves and getting your hands dirty. I know it is easy to say these things, but rather than give money to the poor, what about actually living with them? I reckon that is much more incarnational. To live alongside gives one much more authority to speak out on these matters, even politicians will acknowledge that. So how does the church "live alongside"? Well, I believe that there is still a strong case for the parish priest to live in a parsonage that is within the parish and to be a visible and tangible personage with whom anyone can relate. Now, that is easier said than done, so what about the rest of the parish, what about those who come to church on Sundays and put their money on the plate? No easy answers here, I am afraid and in many ways it's just a case of plodding on hopefully. It will be a very long term project, after all, it could be said that we are still waiting for the "Second Coming". Example is a good teacher, but we have to have people out there who have the ability to relate and who have a personality that can find favour with a community.

Yes, we need academics. We need saintly men and women of prayer, but we need outward going priests who can build up relationships and above all we need bishops who both appreciate this fact and are happy to encourage this process. Not very exciting, but then go and take a look at many of the parishes that make up pastoral life in this country. Quite honestly they are dull with not much sense of community, yet a lively church could well be the catalyst to create a new and dynamic community with benefits for everyone. It is this sort of situation that the church must address and be prepared to put money into. There is no point in just turning away washing ones hands; there are people living in these parishes and for the most part they have no knowledge of the Lord Jesus at all, and I thought that the Church of England was the established church of the land and able to permeate into every nook and cranny! I sincerely hope that I am not wrong.

Chapter 11

BACK TO TRAINS

It is a great shame that Stratford upon Avon is at the end of the line, but at least we do have a station with a reasonable number of trains. It could be far worse, even allowing for the ghastly shuttering that awaits the intrepid day tripper on exiting the platform in 2015/16. Gone are the days when one could be served a three course meal in the restaurant.

There has been much talk about the need to have a direct train to London, but Chiltern Railways have cut the service down to the bone whilst commencing a brand new service from Oxford via the new Bicester Junction and thus dramatically clogging up capacity for trains that start further to the north. In fairness, Stratford station was never built for access to the capital, but for access to Birmingham and also to the south west. I am told that many years ago, there was a direct service from the town to the capital, but it went via the Stratford upon Avon and Midland Junction Line. I am told that it took a very long time. People may feel that the town is the centre of the cultural universe, but they need to face up to certain realities.

A look at the map might be profitable, seeing the direction of the railway line. You can certainly access London by going north east, but there is a stretch of single track with stations and a junction at Hatton onto the main line, all of which help to ensure slow progress! If there was an extension going south west, then there are the connections at Honeybourne to be dealt with, including the construction of a chord and ultimately the doubling of the track from Charlbury to Wolvercote Junction. This latter project has been dismissed by the government and even if a connection at Honeybourne was made and it was possible to access London, I am not too sure that it would be a speedy service and with the insensitive pricing policy of Great Western Railway, most people would not be able to afford it.

I belong to the Gloucestershire, Warwickshire Railway and hopefully one day we might make a connection at Honeybourne, the Cotswold Line promotion group and the Shakespeare Line promotion group. I have therefore, more than a passing interest and there is nothing more I would like to see than the restoration of trains down to Honeybourne from Stratford upon Avon. Needless to say there are the usual *nimby* objections, but what is the main problem here? Not the scarcity of trains and we are not talking about many, but what concerns me is getting either over or under the Evesham Road! Technically very possible, but what about the chaos and especially what about the cost? A business case has been made out, but at the end of the day, it will revolve around what happens at the other end of the line, and that for the most part is out of our control. The Oxfordshire end passes through the constituency of the Prime Minister, but at the moment he is being reminded that the A40 is absolutely clogged up and there is a pressing need to reopen the branch line from Witney to Oxford. I have to say that I suspect this project is more likely to find favour. There are too many disparate groups and individuals who are not working together and until they do and we get ourselves linked up, this worthwhile project will flounder and we will get nowhere down the old branch line.

It never ceases to amaze me as to the number of railway aficionados who just pop up willy nilly and Stratford upon Avon is no exception to the rule. Fortunately some of these appearances have been profitable. There have been some successes, especially the persuasion of the Shakespeare Line Group which has been brought to bear on London Midland Railway for the restoration of a service linking Stratford and Birmingham via Solihull and of course we do have the luxury of some magnificent engines pulling specials from all parts of the country; but what about the turntable, of which much was spoken but little delivered? Yet to be fair, the service into Birmingham is good and the cost is not exorbitant. It would be unfair to blame London Midland concerning the delays in the construction of the footbridge or the proposed retail development; let's hope that eventually we shall have a station to be proud of and that we will continue to both use it and actively promote it.

It is refreshing to be talking about actually adding to the railway stock, rather than taking away even if it is the Heritage Railway sphere of operation. As far as the GWSR is concerned, it is the intention to be running a timetable service into Broadway for the 2018 season. Much work has been carried out at Broadway and track is now being laid. This will bring the total mileage up to close on 15 miles. Now there is a point of discussion here in that there are people who feel that 15 miles is about the farthest you can go on a volunteer based railway. If you try to go further, then everything comes crashing down. I reckon it is close to a multiplier effect. The big boys such as the West Somerset, The North Yorkshire Moors and the Bluebell, can manage a longer distance, but then they do have quite a few full time staff and that makes all the difference. I understand that there have been discussions with interested parties concerning a possible extension to Honeybourne and a very forward looking Network Rail has put in a special platform for us. However I think that the most likely extension would be further into Cheltenham by about another mile through the tunnel, which would make the racecourse station a through station. We shall have to wait and see as there will be the need to consolidate once the route into Broadway has been opened.

But to return to network rail track in the Stratford upon Avon area and the possible extensions into London. I reckon that for the short to medium term we will just have to cope with what we have. Looking at the revised timetable, I note that for the most part, even with a change at Leamington Spa, the timings into Marylebone are faster. What we need to do is to continuously go on at Chiltern to ensure an efficient change over at Leamington Spa and that there are enough seats for those who have come up from Stratford upon Avon. In addition, perhaps a look could be had at the single track between Wilmcote Junction and Hatton Junction and also the need to stop at all three stations. Doubling up the track and removing the need to stop at each and every station could well cut the journey time by a noticeable amount especially if permissions were given for a somewhat faster exit from the platforms. I am sure that a locally constituted rail support group would be advantageous to all parties as long as it would work together and also take a broad view of the possibilities.

I still like to go out for a day on the railways, I can't think of a more civilised manner of travelling and it is not expensive, especially if you invest in a rail card. I picked up this particular "disease" when I was in Alcester and have never recovered to this day. I am grateful to my friends, David, Julian, Vernon and Brian for their support on these occasions and I am sure they will agree with me that we have had a lot of fun.

Invariably, such trips involve getting up at some unearthly hour and making our way to Northfield Station where the parking is free and we could catch the first train out to New Street. Then it was a bacon butty or, if there was time a trip up to Bennett's Hill and Wetherspoons for a cholesterol breakfast. There was still time to catch the first train north in the general direction of Manchester or Liverpool. Occasionally we might change at Crewe and go off to North Wales, but usually we kept going north. On one occasion, we turned off at Carnforth and went up towards Giggleswick where we picked up the famous Settle and Carlisle line. The scenery was out of this world and we managed a first rate lunch in a village pub, close to the line; the landlord even put out copies of the Times and the Yorkshire Post for us to read.

There always seem to be more possibilities up in the northern reaches of our country when it comes to playing at trains. A trip on the daily train into Heysham harbour was interesting; especially when it transpired that it arrived at least half an hour after the daily sailing had departed!!! Then there was a special to Ravenglass from Birmingham behind a heritage mainline electric loco. It became exciting when we arrived at Carnforth and the electric loco came off to be replaced by "Leander", a Jubilee class loco which puffed us round to the narrow gauge railway where special trains had been laid on. The weather was heavenly and the spirit of the Lake District descended upon us.

Occasionally we turned southwards which meant starting from either Ashchurch or Cheltenham. The welsh valleys soon beckoned us and having covered them and the docks area of Cardiff we decided to branch out to Pembroke. After a visit to Carmarthen Castle and the inevitable pub lunch we then took the local train for the coast. On arrival, we were asked to leave the train so that the crew could have a break, so we walked into town and to a supermarket so that we could buy sandwiches for the return journey. Back to the train and it was apparent that we had a drunk on board. The station was also a Real Ale bar and some bottles had accidentally been left out with the inevitable results. This guy soon became restless and wanted more beer, but by that time we were travelling along the line and there was no chance. Then there was a hold up as we had to wait at Tenby to cross with the outward train and this put us in danger of missing our connections which were becoming more and more parlous as our friendly drunk was just getting in the way of everyone. Eventually we arrived at Carmarthen and our friend leapt out of the train to access the buffet and purchase more beer. No luck, as two burly railway staff grabbed him and hauled him back into the train and we got away in record time. Fortunately we made our connections.

Then there was the trip down to Plymouth stopping off at Exeter and ensuring that we made Barnstaple and Exmouth while we were down there. We arrived early in Plymouth so did a deal with a friendly taxi driver to drive us around the sights of the city. There was not time to call at the gin distillery, but we did have a look at the spot where Drake is supposed to have played bowls and then it was time to return to Plymouth station for our trip up to Gunnerslake. This is an incredible journey which takes on almost alpine proportions towards the end. Even with a Devon ranger ticket it is possible to cross over the Tamar at Calstock and into Cornwall before the steep ascent up to Gunnerslake. When you arrive at this lonely outpost it is difficult to comprehend that you are actually on the network. Never mind about that because for the short time before the return journey commences it is well worth appreciating the views which needless to say are first rate. That was certainly a good day out but there were others that took us in a southerly direction including a trip up the four branch lines that link in with Paddington main line. Greenford, Windsor, Marlow and Henley all received visits from us on our perambulations and topped up by a first rate lunch in the shadow of that modest detached and castellated residence which her Majesty is known to inhabit from time to time.

We still have certain targets which we need to achieve and that includes crossing all the London bridges. Mind you we did spend a day on the Croydon tram, the Barking to Gospel Oak line and various others when we must have travelled in close on 30 trains. To date we have not attempted to call at every tube station in one day, I think that old age has caught up with me on that one.

A variation on a theme that has appealed to us is that of trams. Recently we checked out the Nottingham system, which since our visit has expanded and needs another visit and then there was the Sheffield system which greatly impressed us, especially the line which climbs very steeply out of the city and makes off into the countryside. The views on this line are out of this world and it is quite dramatic to look back down on the city and upon where you have just climbed up from. In addition, we have travelled on the Manchester system and this has recently been extended and so too requires further investigation. I think we can leave the Midland metro for the time being and as for the Edinburgh system, I think I would want to wait to ensure that all is running as it should be.

You only have to travel on these modern trams to appreciate how flexible they are and what a disaster it was to have scrapped all those tram cars all those years ago. We never seem to be able to cast our minds forward do we? There is also a cultural point here and that relates to a well entrenched attitude that trains and trams are part of organised transport for the masses as opposed to the freedom to buy a car and go where you like. You can drive off the road but the rails guide you to predetermined places and despite all that is said, I reckon that deep down it clashes with our corporate psyche.

Certainly I do hope we get more trams in the big cities, our continental friends seem to have no problem and it is a pleasure to travel on them.

This chapter is entitled *Back to Trains* so perhaps we should leave trams for the time being and actually go back to some memorable train journeys. I reckon to have travelled on most of the narrow gauge railways in Wales, with just a few small exceptions. I can only just remember a trip on the Vale of Rheidol Railway many years ago, but I certainly remember the great climb up to Devil's Bridge and the waterfall within walking distance. However it was a recent visit to the Welshpool and Llanfair Railway which stirred memories. It is quite easy to get to by train of course. Birmingham, Shrewsbury and then first stop on the Cambrian line. Welshpool gives the impression of being quite a busy market town and it is an enjoyable walk up through the main street. In our case we were hungry and so a cholesterol breakfast was in order, before finding ourselves at Raven Square which is just out of the town on the north side. This is the current terminus, but in the old days, the line went down the town to end up adjacent to the Cambrian line. I can remember on one occasion in the family car having to wait while the engine crossed the road in front of us, but that was many years ago.

It was a great joy and surprise to find that the seller of tickets for the line was a member of the Alcester Railway Circle, so needless to say that rather delayed proceedings and we only just caught the next train. But what a journey! That little engine absolutely hammered up the bank out of Welshpool with commendable power, it was a most impressive performance and ultimately we were able to settle down and enjoy the pastoral scenes that greeted us on our way to Llanfair. This small town/village is not exactly a hub of activity and so we took the next return train after a short recce into the centre.

There is another little railway that I have travelled on myself and that is the Corris. It does not go very far but it nestles in the heart of the Welsh Mountains and deserves as much support as it can muster. It does enjoy very good relations with the Tallylyn which is situated on the other side of the mountain and has the same gauge which has proved useful for special occasions. To my mind the Corris needs some more political muscle as they seem to keep coming up against bureaucracy in their worthy attempt to extend their delightful little line southwards.

I was also a member for some years of the old Welsh Highland (Heritage Railway). I had been appointed as camp chaplain at Butlins and needed to pay in the Sunday collection and it was during my perambulations of Porthmadog, looking for the bank that I discovered this delightful little line and its even more delightful little engine, "Russell" in to which repair fund I have put a reasonable amount of money. This railway is adjacent to the Network Rail Station, just out of town and is well worth a visit. They had a legal battle with the Ffestiniog some years ago, but at least that is now over and relationships seem to be improving at a most agreeable rate. The Old Heritage railway is now invited to link in with the restored Welsh Highland Line and run its trains up into the mountains. I know that this has been much appreciated and has helped to heal some old and festering wounds.

So I reckon it needs to be back to the standard gauge to finish off this chapter. On day excursions we tended to keep away from the eastern seaboard, partly because of timetabling our return journey in one day. On one memorable day we came into and departed from Lincoln on four different routes. It would have been nice to have visited the cathedral, but there just was not time, so we went off to Doncaster for lunch before taking the Grimsby train with the intention of going into the fishing port, but then we found ourselves at Barnetby Junction and as it was the meeting point of three lines, we decided to hop out there and do some serious train spotting! We were not disappointed and were much impressed by the great variety of freight traffic that passed through. There is not much at Barnetby to write home about but at least there is a platform and a few seats.

Back over to the western seaboard and on one occasion we decided to travel on the somewhat eccentric line running from Wrexham to the Wirral peninsula. A rather odd experience, but at least we were able to say that we had now travelled on all the lines that traversed the Wirral, including

Merseyside Electric lines. On another occasion, we had come under this particular line at Flint on our way up to Holyhead which although being a somewhat grim looking port did give us a good day out. We found a pub in the main street with rear views looking out on both the harbour and the railway station. There were large glass viewing panels and the entire room was stepped, just like a football stadium. It was a superb view and we were able to have a good liquid lunch in comfort and do some train and boat spotting from our vantage point.

Southport was a busy little station with two separate lines and it was invigorating to walk down Lord Street and breathe in the sea air. It took me a little time to get used to the compact little electric units on Merseyside, but eventually I got to really enjoy being on them and also appreciate the joy of a little bit of underground railway as we dipped under the Mersey.

There were many other journeys that we made, including a wonderful day trip to Edinburgh, when we arrived spot on time and returned into Birmingham, also on time. We were rewarded with a trip down Princes Street and the Royal Mile, plus a visit to the High Kirk, before hugging the eastern coast all the way down to the Tyne. I just wish that the trams had been in place!

If only. There are many lines that I would have loved to have traversed, but Dr. Beeching and others have conspired to block me on that one. The Great Central, I only managed once, likewise the Midland and Great Northern. I never managed the Somerset and Dorset and I never had so much as a whiff of the Oxford and Cambridge, despite living fairly close by. I was not around when the Lynton and Barnstaple closed down, but I am a member and have travelled on the current one mile line. The future looks rosy and I hope to go back, where the Bristol Channel and the hills of Exmoor make a wonderful backdrop.

Chapter 12

A FUNNY THING HAPPENED!

One of the most important qualities that a priest must have is that of a sense of humour. Life can get pretty grim in the parish and the more characters that we can find, then the better for our blood pressure. Characters/personalities make the world go round and they certainly help in parish life. Many a time in my tribute at a funeral of a well-known and loved parishioner, I have said that he or she must be one of the very last remaining personalities in our community. Even a very basic level of mathematical achievement ought to tell us that it cannot go on forever and soon there will be none.

The fun element was all too evident to appreciate at the time of my first sermon as a clergyman. It was short in length, so much so that the organist was still sitting on the toilet seat behind the organ smoking his cigarette. The churchwarden sprinted up the stairs and banged on the door of the toilet, all of which was heard with much mirth down in the church. We eventually sang the appropriate hymn! On another occasion, I had fully prepared a sermon for the parish mass and after due prayer, I slid out into the centre of the aisle to make my obeisances before climbing into the pulpit. Unfortunately for me, my training incumbent had done exactly the same thing, so there was this slight argument which all could see. The boss won that one, so I kept my sermon for another day.

Then there was my first sermon at Evensong as Vicar of Shottery. Again, it was short in length, which resulted in a very hurried and audible crunching of hardboiled sweets when I announced the next hymn. There were two miscreants, one was a retired undertaker and the other was called Pope!

I had been at Shottery for some years when we decided to hold a parish eucharist in the evening on about four occasions each year. There was one particularly hot and balmy evening when I left the vestry door open which gave direct access to the main body of the church. Our pet dog, Honey was in the habit of going for a stroll around the grounds at about this time and to her delight, access to church was not barred. So, she wandered in and caught the full force of my declaration of forgiveness with an accompanying flourish of a sign of the cross. She looked so surprised and being a Labrador, so concerned when she was rapidly escorted outside.

Shottery may have given the impression of being a sleepy backwater, but we did have our moments and on one particular service there were some sides men on duty who were all for having a little fun. They went to the electricity mains box and turned off the switch for the organ. At this point, Mary Sturch, the organist had arrived and slid into position on the organ stool. She had regaled herself in a scarlet academic gown, with a scarlet mortar board. Having suitably preened herself, she selected which stops she required and then pressed down very firmly on the keys. Nothing happened of course, and there was silence, other than some giggling from within the congregation. Mary was furious and slammed the organist's gate hard against the stalls, before stalking to the back of the church to switch on the current. The giggling burst out into almost uncontrolled mirth. I felt bad about it, but must confess that it was funny.

I cannot remember me ever having any "Vicar of Dibley" moments, but I did not do too badly over the years. Life at Newton Aycliffe could be a bit grim, but there were some notable occasions and all you could do was to laugh. On one occasion, Bishop David Jenkins was in the pulpit, in fact it was at my Institution, when he let rip at the politicians. Mind you he served up his attacks in equal portions so at least they had something to agree about. As I had been instituted on St. Cecelia's day in November, it was not long before Christmas, and I was warned that I might have some unruly customers, especially as some of the locals would want to check me over. It did not quite work out that way, but I did need the assistance of the police. As it happened, there were some very attractive ladies sitting in the front row and behind them were some boorish and very drunk lads who proceeded to intimately attend to them, by trying to lift their skirts. I can put up with a lot, including noise, but I had reached the end of my tether when suddenly a very serious looking churchwarden, accompanied by his son who was an off duty policeman, walked quickly down the central aisle and just lifted these guys and carried them out. It was brilliant. No aggro and we had no more disturbances.

On another occasion, there had been a supplementary parade organised by the Royal British Legion. It was amusing because it was very much like a "Little and Large Show", a very big Standard Bearer, with a diddy Inspecting Officer namely the Earl of Scarborough, who trooped along behind wearing his bowler and carrying his brolly. He was absolutely charming and got on very well with the Mayor who was certainly very much to the left of the political spectrum. It transpired that they both enjoyed a cigarette and so clouds of smoke sealed a very enjoyable afternoon.

During my time at Alcester, the influence of what was originally a Roman settlement ensured a long history from which to pinpoint certain events. Since the middle ages, Alcester had been dominated by its medieval church tower and at one particular Civic Service I had been talking to the Mayor and Councillors before the service about a possible leak in the roof. For once, I was pleased to experience a heavy rain storm and so the roof leaked and the collection was good.

I was told by Padre Jim Symonds that when he was in his first parish, he had a similar problem when there was a big wedding blessing. The difference was that in his congregation were a lot of very wealthy Arabian Sheiks who were "persuaded" to part with their money by some "hired heavies" who were at the beck and call of the boss man! Some people have all the luck!

There was a gorgeous brass candelabra suspended above the central aisle in Alcester Church. You could absolutely guarantee that at a Parade Service that it would be struck by at least one of the processional flags. It was just a question of which organisation was to blame, but it was all taken in good fun and it became almost a badge of authenticity that you could claim to have struck the candelabra! I know for a fact that on at least one occasion the Royal British Legion, no less, committed this cardinal sin. But then that is all part of the great fun of ministry in a well developed community like Alcester.

I was in London one day for a meeting at USPG (now US) and as it did not start until after lunch, I was able to slip into All Saints, Margaret Street for a spiritual high! Now the first thing you appreciate about All Saints is that it is very dark. Why? Well, all those years ago, there was a legal judgement by the Privy Council as to the use of candles in church. The decision was that they could not be used to aid devotion, but they could be used to light up the church, so that you could see what you were doing. Needless to say, this led to all the Anglo Catholic Churches being built to ensure that they were very dark inside.

In the old days, the first things that you would see would be three confessionals and you could sense a very definite spiritual feel about the place. It has changed a little since then, but there are still the confessionals, and one of them was being used when I called. What amazed me was that roars of laughter were emitting from it and a little boy was playing with his toys, just a few feet away. What had happened was that a young mum wanted to make her confession and this was the only way that she could do so. It certainly was a change from the old days and then to cap it all, at the lunchtime mass, the assistants just wore tatty jeans and open neck shirts. The saints of All Saints would be turning in their graves.

However if you want to experience what All Saints is especially good at then I suggest going to Solemn Evensong with Benediction. I recall this choir of young ladies who wore a vestment like a soutane with the sleeves removed. They were very graceful and sang like linnets. All Saints has always had a very good reputation for music and even the Church Times was minded on one occasion to say that going there was to experience a glimpse of heaven. Praise indeed!

At the other end of the scale, I remember an evensong down at the Elephant and Castle. We were on mission training and the service was being conducted by Ernie Smith, the Reader, who incidentally was the father of my predecessor as a curate in Coventry. Ernie had a traditional south London accent and I could not help grinning when he started with those immortal words "O Lord, open thou our lips". Most of us had Oxbridge type accents, so we stuck out like a sore thumb, but it did not take long for us to integrate with the local community and we came to love them dearly and they, us!

Talking of the South Bank. I did go to Southwark Cathedral on a couple of occasions for a big service. It is a delightful little cathedral, and although a bit on the liberal side as far as liturgy is concerned, it has the big advantage of being free entrance, unlike St. Pauls on the other side of the river.

I had attended the ordination of a friend of mine and we all retired to the George for liquid refreshment afterwards. The father-in-law of my pal, who just happened to be a licensee down in Somerset, lined up the drinks and since this took some time, he started to swig down his ale and so by the time the order was complete and it was time to pay, it was also time for him to have his glass topped up. I only just realised what he was up to. Clearly this was an old trick of his and nobody in the family has ever cottoned on to it. The pub is owned by the National Trust and is a gem.

Back to parish life and its many amusing moments. One thing I cannot abide is looking at miserable christians. Perhaps that is a contradiction, but I still see plenty around even to this day. What is their problem? Why are they coming to church and making other people miserable as well? When I was at theological college, the students emptied out into the Cathedral Close after the paschal mysteries to find a bevy of miserable looking Christians on their way to the 8.00am Holy Communion. I must admit that we were a bit irreverent, but even shouts of "Smile. Jesus loves you!" had no effect. Incidentally this was Easter Morning and you would think that even eight o'clockers who are a very special breed might at least have permitted themselves a smile on that most joyful of days.

So in parish life I would almost as a matter of policy try and break up a gathering of miseries with a remark such as "If the devil could cast his net". It worked most times but there were the occasional dissenters. Still, there were other ways to get people laughing such as when I passed the local M.P. a German bomb in church. He soon passed it on when he realised what it was. In fact it was a family heirloom and had been picked up by my father during the Bristol Blitz. I used to bring it out from time to time for very special occasions.

But the best occasion in church which really got the children's attention was when I persuaded the landlady of the Holly Bush Hotel to cook a special chicken dish on a skillet and then when it was steaming and smoking she brought it into church. Mind you I had told the uniformed organisations that they were to close their eyes and to keep them closed. The idea was to cast one's minds back to a special meal which even now they could almost still smell, let alone taste. I then ruined the christian message by eating the chicken myself in front of some very eager Beavers and Cubs.

We also had a lot of fun when our French twinning counterparts from Vallet in the Rhone Valley paid us one of their visits. Needless to say there were diplomatic niceties to be observed and sensitivities as well. On one visit, our French friends felt that they really all ought to be terribly British by buying a tie and wearing it for the benefit of their British hosts. That was a laugh because very few of the home team had actually put on a tie and it could be said that they had caught the French disease of being casual and laid back. But then our French friends showed their true Gallic tendencies when I had taken some of them up the church tower for a better view of the Town. Horror of horrors, before I had time to say "Entente Cordiale" some of our French friends had climbed up onto a very exposed, and to my mind, dangerous part of the roof and were virtually swinging there. I was having kittens and they did not seem to see that there might be a problem.

On the other hand our French friends were most generous and as they came from the Muscadet region of France, they brought enough of that particular wine for Alcester to enjoy for a very long time. I am not a dry white wine aficionado, but it is surprising how soon you change your taste buds when it is diplomatic to do so. Vive La France!

There was fun in abundance to be had at the local hospital in Stratford upon Avon. I have very happy memories of the old wooden huts and the general wartime flavour. Many people today would be horrified at such facilities, but I am not aware of any deaths that could be put down to that. It was a particularly rustic situation as the wards were separated from the operating theatre by an access road into the cattle market and this track was well used, especially on market days, so there were times when patients on trolleys had to wait their turn as well. It was an even bigger problem during inclement weather because somehow or other, the patient still had to be wheeled safely for the surgeons to do their work. They got round this problem by erecting protective boards along the side of the trolley and then draping a blanket over the poor unfortunate individual who ended up being in a mobile tunnel. In addition to crossing the road there was also the possible dilemma of going close to the mortuary and just hoping that the undertakers had not chosen that moment to make a delivery. And of course, in the background there was also the mooing and baaing which came from the market.

Talking of the morgue, reminds me of the famous occasion when the undertakers came to collect a body for a funeral and went away with the wrong body. It only came to light a little while later when a second collection discovered the error. Panic! I am told that Eric Collett the local manager sat down in his chair at the office, pulled the drawer out from his desk, placed a bottle of sherry on top of the desk and dispensed himself a couple of draughts of the fortified liquid. Having knocked them back, he phoned up his old friends at the police station and explained the problem.

No problem said they and promptly sent out a police car which set up a road block and the errant hearse was subsequently turned back! It took some time to live that one down, but the next-of-kin did not know about it and everyone breathed a sigh of relief.

I had the honour one Friday of being visited by a Bishop. Although it wasn't quite like that, I recorded an Episcopal Visitation in my register. The wife of the Bishop of Sodor and Man (to give him his slightly unfortunate title) had been admitted to hospital and wanted to have communion, as did her husband. I was down on the wards when I got the call and hurried off to make my obeisances. Having genuflected and kissed the episcopal ring (which clearly went down very well), I was introduced to Bishop Vernon Nicholls, who in years to come became a good friend as he retired to Shottery. We then got into an argument, because I said that as he was a bishop and I was a mere priest, he should pronounce the absolution. No, you do it was the firm reply. There was no point in arguing, Bp Vernon was clearly in the habit of getting his own way.

I suppose though, I tended to get my own way because I was chaplain and got on well with the staff and especially with matron who was a practising Methodist and very supportive. Although not even she could shift a room full of men out from where I had hoped to have a special communion service as the usual room was having repairs. There had been a mix up in room bookings, so there was no point in making a fuss. Although the porters who inhabited their lodge almost next door took a special delight in winding me up about the incident. Never mind, all in a day's work.

It is perhaps appropriate that while I was making my very last visit to the hospital as chaplain and saying goodbye to some very old friends, when a steam hauled excursion drew into Stratford upon Avon station and disgorged hordes of day trippers. I cannot be too sure, but I think the loco was "Duchess of Hamilton". This was certainly a very regular visitor and gave me something to talk about down on the geriatric wards, where many of the patients had happy memories of through expresses at Stratford all those years ago.

Turning to the cathedral, I recall the day of my ordination to the diaconate when we were led into the service by Archdeacon Ted Taylor, also known as "Canon Fodder" with the immortal words "Forward Men". I have never really liked the cathedral as a building and I suppose that part of that is because of me being fairly traditional by nature, however once I had been installed as an Honorary Canon, I was given a very comprehensive tour by the Precentor and discovered some fascinating information which put the cathedral into a better perspective as far as I was concerned. In any case I well remember the excitement of holding my girlfriend's hand whilst watching a twin rotor blade helicopter drop into place a cross on the top of the metal tower. So I could go back a few years!

At that time I reckon there was something wrong with the organ as it was often difficult to hear, but today the sound engineers have certainly sorted out the problem and it makes a very merry and distinctive sound.

When I went back to the cathedral after one year to be ordained priest, the ordaining Bishop was that delightful Australian, Bishop John Mackie. Now, he was great fun and popular with the clergy, but he had one big fault and that was a complete lack of liturgical sensitivity. The altar looked like a junk heap once he had been up there and he used to knock things over as he moved from one station to another. Despite this, we had all been invited to concelebrate with Bishop John and yet I had the feeling that we were being watched. Yes, we were! By the Precentor, who was looking like a disgusted hawk as he saw the altar unfold to the machinations of this unruly Australian. In fact he moved in and did some tidying up during the consecration prayer and Bishop John did not even notice.

Now, concluding this chapter brings me to my final thoughts to draw this unexpected sequel to an end. So what about a train joke? Clean, I promise.

This can be told anywhere on the railway map and can be amended to suit particular railways, stations and/or engines. It goes as follows:

The Almighty was seated on his magnificent throne on the platform of a very big railway station. An A4 class pacific loco came in being driven by Nigel Gresley. "Who are you?" asked the Almighty. "I am Sir Nigel Gresley of the London and North Eastern Railway and I designed and built this beautiful beast." Suitably impressed, Gresley was invited to take a seat at the right hand on high and a shunter dragged the A4 off to the sheds. Next came a Coronation class with Bill Stanier at the controls. "Who are you?" asked the Almighty? "I am Sir William Stanier F.R.S. of the London Midland and Scottish Railway and I designed and built this beautiful beast." Again, the Almighty was suitably impressed and Bill Stanier joined the illustrious few on the top table. Off went the Coronation class to the sheds. There was then a very lengthy pause and clearly the Almighty was getting fed up, but at last there was a distant noise and soon could be heard the movement of a rusty tank engine which ultimately appeared around the corner looking very unkempt and grotty. Out jumped Churchward of eternal fame. "Who are you?" asked the Almighty somewhat dismissively. The reply to which was as follows, "I am George Jackson Churchward of the Great Western Railway and you are sitting on my seat." This little story went up and down the line at Winchcombe very quickly.

Chapter 13

COMING TO THE END OF THE LINE

As most of you seem to know, I do not approve of long sermons. To my mind, if I cannot make my point in about 6-8 minutes, then I ought to sit down and shut up. There are too many people around who like the sound of their own voice. I just hope I am not developing into a writing equivalent. This last two months has given me a chance to do something different for a change. Hilary quite rightly told me that I really ought to find something else to do now that illness had thrown a spanner in the works.

Being diagnosed with atrial fibrillation got me thinking and rather knocked me off my perch. I need to rethink and re-plan. I am the sort of person who likes to organise my life for many months ahead and finds it difficult to cope when other factors combine to destroy all the best laid plans.

However there are benefits, such as the title of this missive. Part of the manifestation of atrial fibrillation in my case was that I began puffing like an old grampus. Well, as I like my steam trains, this got me off to a good start. *The Puffing Parson!* I am just hoping that I do not get into trouble with any of my clerical brethren for nicking their prized title. I am still thinking about a secondary title as I write these last few chapters, but eventually there will have to be some reference to a branch line or coming to the end of the line. But what shall I find? Well, speaking as a railway enthusiast, there would have to be at least one steam railway awaiting me in heaven and preferably it would be Great Western in its orientation and as I adore a cholesterol breakfast, there would have to be the facilities for bacon and eggs on the coal shovel. If I am really fussy, then I would love to have a narrow gauge railway as well. Yet, despite my love of all those gorgeous little trains in Wales, I have to remember that I come from the West Country and therefore it has to be the Lynton and Barnstaple railway in all its entirety going up over Exmoor and causing the red deer to scamper out of the way.

Finally, just to be on the safe side, perhaps a modest Real Ale micro brewery. All sorts of titles for beers come to mind such as, Puffing Parson Old Ale, Rector's Revenge. The list could go on ad infinitum. But I digress. I must start to finish off, if that is not a contradiction. So, I shall use the analogy of a good meal. At the end of such an event I would normally like a decent brandy or even if possible an Armagnac, after which I can go home and sleep well. Therefore, one or two final stories that bring back very happy memories should do the trick and then I can lay up my pen, or in this modern age, my computer keyboard and feel that I have done what I should have done. There most certainly will not be a sequel to a sequel. I am not even sure that is a possibility anyway. I suppose that if I was to be dragged out of retirement and persuaded that a distant diocese wanted me as their bishop, that might just justify a sequel, but a bookie would doubtless not even quote odds, and who could blame him?

*　　*　　*

Those last thoughts and memories – An interlude

It has been an inexpressible joy and privilege to be a priest and to be able to minister in ways that other people are just not fortunate enough to be able to copy. Despite there being many sad times, there have been far more joys. I have been able to look in on the most intimate part of a marriage service, when a couple pledge their troth one to another, and when they look at each other as they slip the rings on to the fingers. Nobody else sees this moment, it is a wonderful joy and pleasure and privilege. Likewise to be able to hold an infant and wonder as you baptise the much wanted child of a couple who have been wanting a baby for years and have almost given up hope. But unfortunately some of these joys can turn to tragedies and you are there to stand by people in their hour of need.

There are times when I need to get away and find some space and some solitude. There is a definite need to recharge your spiritual batteries. Some go to monasteries or convents for that extra spiritual quality. Some go to retreat houses. We are all different and may well need to seek out the right place. I have been to Devon, to the Society of Martha and Mary situated at Sheldon in the Teign valley. I always go by train and with the benefit of my rail card; I treat myself to a bit of luxury and go First Class to Exeter St.

David's station and then take a taxi to my final destination. Here I could walk, I could pray, I could contemplate, I could talk to the community, I could do my own thing, but I always came away feeling very much better both physically and spiritually. But you will never guess, because there is a railway at the bottom of the garden. It is called the Teign Valley Railway and is based around the old Christow Station. There is about 400 yards of standard gauge track and a rusty diesel 02 shunter. Needless to say, on my walks I inevitably wondered off in that direction and examine the various artefacts that are on show.

But, back home: I have missed out on various GWR activities these last few months. I think that playing Santa has always been the most enjoyable really, because of the magical feeling and the looks of wonderment from the children. I hope to go back to that next year and I shall certainly be able to carry on as a farmer doing wartime evacuations. That is great fun and there are also sufficient breaks for me to at least sit down and have lunch. Lastly of course will be the Meeting and the Greeting of coach parties and the only worry here is really as to how much the party want to enter into the real spirit of the occasion. No two people are the same, and likewise as to groups. I have only had one particularly taciturn group. But even they said a warm thank you at the end. Needless to say, I have shamelessly promoted the railway with my own church connections, with the result that Santa, cream teas, bacon rolls, shed visits etc are now part of the local ecclesiastical stock in trade. My next project is to see if I can persuade the Ecclesiastical Press to underwrite the cost of a Clergy Express. That could be interesting!

Chapter 14

MEMORABLE TRAIN JOURNEYS

My engagement to Hilary when I was a curate provoked enough positive comment, but there were gasps when it transpired that for our honeymoon we would do the grand tour of Switzerland by train, very much in the spirit of our Edwardian forefathers. Chapelfields was very much an upper working class parish and that sort of trip would not normally be on the menu for most people. However, we had both saved and felt that a special occasion like a honeymoon deserved a special trip.

Once we arrived in Basle it was clear that Swiss efficiency would be the order of the day; because at no time did we ever carry our bags into the hotels, they were already waiting for us in our bedrooms. A short coach trip from the airport brought us to the main railway station where before we knew what was happening we were sitting down in the restaurant and tucking into a nourishing meal. It was interesting to see that the restaurant manager was actually looking out for our tour party and as soon as we came through the door, the efficiency drive swung into action. We eventually reached Interlaken after a very scenic journey and booked into our hotel. Next morning, as the weather was good we took the decision to go up the Jungfrau. It was the right decision, because on subsequent days the weather deteriorated considerably.

You have to take your hat off to the Swiss. Where there is a mountain, then the Swiss will either build a railway up it or inside it. Eventually we arrived at Kleine Scheidegg which is the col where you change trains and gauge for another railway which actually takes you up inside the mountain. It is an amazing experience and there is even a station half way up so that you can hop out and view the snowfields below through specially constructed windows. On arrival at the summit station, you find that there are even two platforms there, plus appropriate signalling arrangements.

After a few days we took the train for Montreux, which involved another change of gauge up in the mountains and then a dramatic drop down to the shores of Lake Geneva. We were now on the Main line and the trains were big, powerful and fast. When we departed we were told that our group must stand at a predetermined position on the platform and not move. When the train came in, a door would open and all we had to do was to get in. No questions asked, just do as you are told. It worked well and within seconds we were being whisked off in the direction of the Italian border.

Perhaps the most hair raising of our trips was up Mount Pilatus on our penultimate day. The railway boasted that it had never had an accident throughout its long history which exceeded 100 years. We had no problems, but I was amazed to read in the papers a few weeks later after our return, that the Mount Pilatus Railway had its first accident ever, a few days after our journey; fortunately no injuries. But what a railway! When you approach the summit station, the train is held just outside and has to wait for the signals to change and for the points to be switched. The train then slots into one of three platforms, which are all built at an angle of at least 45 degrees. The big gondola from one peak to another and the little gondolas over the delightful alpine meadows were child's play in comparison.

Some years later we determined to cross over to France under the channel and this was a great experience, even if the facilities at both Waterloo and Gare du Nord were somewhat basic. Once in Paris I had the time of my life playing trains on the Metro. It is a wonderful network and the French seem to be able to extend the lines and construct the extensions without all the long and drawn out consultation periods that we seem to like. Although in fairness to the London Underground, which admittedly does have its occasional strike problem, when the French have a strike, they sure have a strike. Ours is like a mole hill, theirs is like a mountain.

Our next venture under the channel was to Bruges and the opportunity to view the World War I battlefields. This time the departure was from St. Pancras. "Vive la difference" I am told that even the French were impressed when it first opened. But there was a problem on the outward journey because the train in front of us broke down and had to be dragged out of the tunnel. We therefore spent some time under the sea before moving off again. At least there was the odd glass of wine. Once we had arrived in Brussels, I soon appreciated the benefit of travelling in this manner, because your eurostar ticket is valid anywhere on the Belgian railways for the rest of the day. What an excellent way to encourage tourism. What would the chances be over here, I ask myself? Zero!

Our most recent trip under the sea was to Avignon three years ago in order to celebrate my retirement. I would strongly advocate this trip, it is delightfully relaxing and the time just slips away. The service was only operating on Saturdays during the summer months, with one train each way and about a six hour journey in total. Basically you get on the train in London and get off at Avignon. No changes at all. The second class seating is extremely comfortable and the only criticism I would have would be that of very high prices in the buffet, but that is inevitable, so you get round that on the return journey by stocking up with delicious French baguettes and plastic bottles of wine – so much cheaper. There was only one stop on the return journey and that was for a crew change at Lille. I am glad we did not get off there as both the station and the platforms looked like a concrete jungle.

But the rest of the journey is pure delight especially as you follow the valley of the River Marne and make for Mediterranean climes. You can certainly tell when you are down in the southern reaches because you start to see lots of sun flowers. I was immediately impressed by the number of fields with these stunning flowers just swaying in the breeze. It made me think of the great French Impressionist painters.

And then, on arrival you can see the famous bridge and the papal palace. It is a delightful city, very compact and the railway station is just over five minutes' walk from the city centre. Emerging from the first gate of the castellated walls the wide avenue leads you to the heart of the city. When you finally leave Avignon by train, you get that incredible view that tells you that you must return one day. I must do so, as it is delightfully laid back and totally unlike northern France. And, by the way, watch out for the Mistral.

We also like to visit a Heritage Railway when on holiday, and of course this could be anywhere, but we did have the opportunity to take our first out of school time holiday this last September and saved ourselves a cool £200 in the process. You can see why taking one's children out of school during normal school time is such a hot potato at the moment, and I do have some sympathy here, especially when it is clearly working arrangements that prohibit a family from going on holiday at any normal time. We had decided to go to the Isle of Wight, thinking it would be relatively quiet, but no such luck. It was still very busy and clearly many of the Silver Service Brigade of which we were now members, had decided to do likewise.

It was decided to go to church on the Sunday and then make our visit, so off to Godshill for Solemn Mass and then onto Havenstreet where we looked around a recently opened museum of very high quality. Ultimately we got onto a steam train bound for Wootton and then by return to Smallbrook Junction and returning to Havenstreet. It was a delight to just sit back and soak up the scenery as we chugged along through woods and very green fields.

But of course there is another railway on the Isle of Wight and that is the electrified line running between Shanklin and Ryde Pierhead. With fairly ancient London Transport Tube Stock, it is quirky to say the least, but it does rattle along and its time keeping is impeccable. I believe that there are plans for steam trains to run along on parallel track from Smallbrook Junction all the way to the Pier, but that is very much in the future.

Another line which we enjoy going on and especially if we are able to take the grandsons, is the North Norfolk Line, also known as the Poppy Line, running from Sheringham to Holt. This is the line made famous by the hilarious goings on of the *Dads Army* Platoon when they had to give a Royal salute and then ended up getting drowned as the engine went over the water troughs. It must have been a great joy when eventually after much discussion and form filling the connection with Network Rail was reinstated and a steam train came all the way through from Norwich.

The Poppy Line is much loved by North Country parishes that go down to Walsingham for a long weekend pilgrimage and then like to go to the seaside on the Saturday. Mind you, it's impossible to keep everyone happy because invariably there are moans if the steam engine happens to be "Oliver Cromwell" of the Standard Britannia Class. For the uninitiated, Oliver Cromwell has always been a big bête noir of the Anglo Catholic movement.

We have also enjoyed the South Devon Railway, despite there being a fairly long walk at Totnes to the Heritage Station and then there is the incomparable Kingswear line from Paignton with its magnificent views of the Torbay beaches and ultimately, the River Dart. One of the best views in England is to come down the steep hill in Dartmouth, past the Naval College and then look out over the estuary when a steam hauled train is leaving. It is absolutely idyllic. Dartmouth must be one of the very few towns with a current railway Station, but no railway. However I am taking a broad view of what a current railway station really is. In Dartmouth it is now a cafe, but in the old days, you could buy your ticket there, and then take the ferry over to Kingswear and finally the train to London.

Last March, we spent a weekend with relatives near Camberley and as their grandson worked on the Mid Hants Line, also known as the Watercress Line, we had an enjoyable day which started at Alton. Here there is a direct connection with network rail. It is possible to come in from London on the electrified line, to cross over the platform and to depart on a steam train. What a wonderful arrangement! It is rumoured that the CEO of the South Western Trains works as a volunteer. Anyway, irrespective of that, it is a delightful line and full of Southern cheer! We were treated to Schools Class and Lord Nelson Class power.

Still, there is one other way of enjoying yourself on a Heritage Railway and that is to charter a train for a private function. I could not run to a Steam engine, but did manage to find the money to charter a Heritage Diesel Electric Multiple Unit to celebrate my 70th birthday. In fairness, it is quite reasonable and I reckon that there is more money that could be made by the various railways if they wanted to develop this market. I booked a complete run over the railway and stopping off for a cream tea at Winchcombe Station. It is possible to arrange for certain extras, for example the attendance of Peter and Moira, our resident musicians who led us in a sing-along. It also doesn't take too much trouble to arrange for the Carriage Works to be open, also the Signal Box and Model Railway.

I can particularly recommend this sort of afternoon out when there are grandchildren around, because the volunteer staff go to amazing lengths to entertain them, including waving the green flag, blowing the whistle and sounding the horn. I entertained about 110 guests and there was plenty of room on the three car unit. Fortunately for me, the unit had just been made up from two to three cars, although we would still have managed to squeeze in.

Anyway, it is time to make the final approach to the buffers and we now swing onto the branch line for the last time.

Chapter 15

THE FINAL APPROACH
TO THE BUFFERS

The signalman has pulled the points off and now I find myself on the branch line. I must confess that I find branch lines fascinating, not that there are many around today. Being very English, they give smaller communities the opportunity to take part in wider affairs and feel part of a greater whole. There is a delightful description by Aldous Huxley in *Crome Yellow* as follows: "Bole, Tritton, Spavin Delawarr, Knipswich for Timpany, West Bowlby and Camlet-on-the-Water". The train snorts into its final station and you have been for a ride in the depths of the English Countryside. Hence my love of Winchcombe station.

How long will this branch line last? Some give the impression of going on for ever, while others are short and sharp such as Stourbridge Junction to Stourbridge Town. Incidentally, well worth a detour to experience the people carrier! However it is time to do some serious thinking as I enter my eighth decade and so, music and literature come to mind. What would I want with me to listen to in my solitary station? A sort of land locked *Desert Island Discs*. Well, I would certainly want some Gilbert and Sullivan, the song, *I have a song to sing oh* is great, but I might still like the overtures to either *Yeoman of the Guard* or *Iolanthe*. Then there would be the famous organ symphony and toccata by Widor. Having played the church organ myself, I know that there are plenty of organists who think they can play this piece, but not many who really can do so. Not too fast either, but it brings back memories of final services in Rugby School Chapel. The overture to *Rienzi* by Wagner would stir me from my lethargy, followed by the *Coronation March* by Meyerbeer which brings back the memories of our wedding when Hilary walked down the aisle to marry me. If I ever had any doubts about the resurrection then the *Easter Hymn* from Cavellaria Rusticana would soon dispel them and then the exquisite duet from the Pearl Fishers, which I have actually sung! Choices, choices, but I would finish off with the *Pomp and Circumstance March* by Elgar, No.4. Not, *Land of Hope and Glory* which I cannot abide. No.4 was the slow march at Rugby when the cadets marched onto the Close for the Annual Inspection. Last but not least, some more organ music and yet again by Widor. Not so famous, but it has happy memories for me and is the *Marche Pontificale*. Well that ought to keep me fairly happy, but what about literature?

I am not sure whether a castaway has a mandatory copy of the bible but I will naturally have it and I would beg for a supplementary text, a compendium of the writings of the early fathers of the church who in effect were the very first commentators on the scriptures. They come from what is called the patristic period and I have spent some fascinating hours studying Cyprian, Irenaeus, Origen, Clement of Rome, Cyril of Jerusalem, to name but a few. It is refreshing to read these commentaries and feel that you are virtually there and in on the act. And finally, what would I like for entertainment? It would have to be the complete cycle of the *Barchester* series. Despite appearances, I still reckon there is a lot that is right about *Barchester*.

I still would like to sing again, at a reasonable level, and it would be from *"Les Miserables"* the song, *"let the people sing"*. But that may be pushing the boat out too much. However, I would also like another crack at the duet from the Pearl Fishers and possibly Cavellaria Rusticana, which I find to be so evocative. I suspect that life is going to be more sedentary in the future and I must confess to enjoying much more reading than in the past. The period of the Plantagenets is what interests me. They were fairly determined, aggressive and assertive when they were not fighting. Not necessarily trustworthy, but they did certainly make a big difference to this country and so much of what is in place nowadays as far as government machinery is concerned as well as general attitudes, can safely be put down to their reign. I do not think that now is the time to discuss the business of when the Plantagenet dynasty actually came to an end. I tend to go for Bosworth Field and the killing of Richard III, but others would subscribe to the view that Henry IV finished it off when he seized the throne from Richard II. I reckon you pays your money and you takes your pick. It is the same with the suggestion that Edward II was not actually murdered but was promptly moved out of the country and ended up on the

French/German borders (as we would know it today), where it is believed that Edward III actually met his father again.

I have listed the railways that I would like to visit. But my mind still wanders in the direction of the Highlands as, other than the Fort William to Mallaig and the Crianlarich to Oban, I have not been on any of the remaining lines and would dearly love to. Also, I would like to go on the branch lines down in Cornwall, having just sampled the Falmouth branch on the one occasion.

No, I think my time will be taken up with some sort of work with the GWR and by continuing to be a priest who would make himself available to other priests who might just want to come and talk things over or even to just let off steam! That might surprise some of you. I can assure you that clergy can be quite emotional at times and get themselves very worked up. If you don't believe me then go along to a clergy cricket match and you will see what I mean, LBW decisions are challenged ad infinitum! I will be delighted to give details of any local fixtures, because I still get involved with them and still arrange the fixtures. If you do come along, make sure you stay to the end, because there are always one or two beefy characters who will want to swig down a couple of pints, if not more! No names mentioned but they are great fun.

But getting back to making myself available. The problem is that nobody has called me! What is the matter with me, I ask myself? Well, I understand that many retired priests like me have experienced the same relative negativity, perhaps it is just a perceived culture that applies to anyone who has retired? A colleague of mine was telling me that retired GPs have a wealth of experience that they would be happy to make available to younger colleagues, but nothing happens and nobody calls. It seems to be such a waste, but on the other hand is it that the world is advancing in knowledge that much quicker? I can see dangers there and a very definite theological argument. But as I have said countless times, most of my friends and contacts know where I live or at least how to get hold of me.

So, the train is now rapidly approaching the station and the signal box is in sight. Don't panic, Mr. Mainwaring! Immediately that reminds me in these days of advanced domestic technology, that there are plenty of television programmes that I like to see repeated. Starting with Dad's Army, I have the complete set of DVDs and can never miss an opportunity to work a story into one of my sermons. It is absolutely classic and I never tire of seeing any of the series. I suspect that most would agree with me that the scene with the U Boat Commander was out of the top drawer as was the time when Wilson told Mainwaring that the Golf Club was rather particular as to who they admitted to membership!

I also take great pleasure in watching anything with Ronnie Barker appearing in it, whether it is *Porridge* or *Open All Hours*. I have American friends from Alabama who own a country retreat which they let out to family and friends. There is a television set, but no television connection, instead there is a large collection of Ronnie Barker DVDs. At least the Americans appreciate our sense of humour.

I also happen to love *It Ain't Half Hot Mum* but you don't see it around nowadays. I suspect that it fails the inevitable PC Test. Last but not least, there is *Only Fools and Horses* which I believe to be fast approaching the level of greatness. I just love a situation which you often find down at the Nags Head. That is my type of scene and I absolutely revel in it. Trigger and Boycie really make a situation like that and without them it would be sadly lacking.

The nearest that I have ever got to that sort of situation was admittedly in South London, in the Elephant and Castle area, when we were on mission training. Me and my pal sniffed out a pub down the backstreets where we were very warmly welcomed. There happened to be a piano and as many of our group were well trained in the musical arts, we had the inevitable sing-along. One evening, the landlord served up pigs' trotters and the inevitable bowl of fat prawns which we devoured. There were tears all round when we took our leave of our new found friends. I really thought that we had brought the church into the lives of the people who we really ought to be serving, many of them did not know anything about the church and about Jesus.

A few days later, I was returning through the back alleys having had a session with the South London Industrial Mission and as I was a little peckish, I invested in a portion of chips. Suddenly a young lad on a brand new bike cycled up to me in great haste and said "Hey mate, give us a chip." I ignored the request and kept walking, but this lad kept persisting and once again he said, "Come on Mister, give us a chip!" It was then I realised what had happened. The lad had been given a new bike to keep him quiet while his parents went out to do other things. It was up to him to feed himself and he clearly had no money and had probably been locked out of his house until later.

I promptly gave him the rest of my chips and his face lit up like a giant candle. It also gave me the background to my first ever sermon. I remember it well! Back at our quarters, I related my experience and I reckon from the response that I got, it was a wonderful missionary opportunity which fortunately had not been turned aside.

The train is now slowing down and drawing into the platform and I do see a stationmaster, but unfortunately he is not wearing a top hat. Never mind. All change, or in my case, no change as I am not going anywhere in particular. Perhaps I should change after all, the Blessed John Henry, Cardinal Newman once said that to change is to grow. I like that, it is so true. The main argument would just be, to what degree we should change. Shades of grey again.

I have to admit that just sitting down at Winchcombe Railway Station on Platform 1 is for me the height of luxury. Not much might pass through, in fact nothing might appear, but on the other hand, something might and it makes it all worthwhile. There is plenty of time. It is also time for me to do something which is more akin to my profession and I call to mind the words of Sister Elaine from the Holy Name sisters all those years ago when she made me a cope and said that now she was back in the Mother House she could concentrate on the most important work of all, and needless to say that is the work of prayer. Sounds a bit pious I know. I cannot help that. Incidentally the motto of my old School at Rugby is, "Orando laborando", which means, by praying and by working etc. I still think of Sister Elaine whenever I put on my cope and also that she designed it on the back of a cigarette packet. May she rest in peace and rise in glory.

I recite the Daily Office twice each day and also read from the writings of the early fathers and until my illness, was available to help out as and when required, although I did pledge my first loyalty to my former parish of Shottery. Up until then, I had been over to Coventry a few times to help out in some of the more down to earth parishes. I thoroughly enjoy going there. I have told them that I do not want a fee and I do not want any expenses. Quite honestly they do not have much money and I would rather they kept it so that they can keep going. Now that I am almost fully recovered from my illness, I shall renew my availability and perhaps renew the spark which remains within me, but which has not really come to life of late, other than the occasional splutter. I need a bit of resurrection to liven me up and that reminds me of what I said to the National President of Rotary a few years ago, I believe in a good death, a decent burial and a glorious resurrection! Give me the resurrection any day. But also, give me the strength to change if I must, and to change with a smile on my face. I just cannot abide miserable christians. In many ways I would prefer the happy sinner rather than the pious saint (on a steam locomotive of course)!

On Wednesday, June 29th, 2016 the Feast of St. Peter, Apostle and Martyr in the evening I shall celebrate 40 years as a Priest by concelebrating the Holy Eucharist with my colleagues in Shottery St. Andrew's, Church. I am looking forward to the day immensely. Deus Volenti!

BY THE SAME AUTHOR

The Fiery Canon – The Ramblings of a Rustic Rector

David Capron traces his family roots back to Huguenot times and then into West Somerset and Devon where an ancestor made a name for himself as a Poet. The family has always had strong connections with the Fire Brigade, especially in the West Country, Oxfordshire and Warwickshire. The move to Rugby where David went to the famous School was instrumental in the initial sowing of the seeds of vocation to become a priest. The struggles at college and then finally ordination in Coventry Cathedral led to the life of a parish priest in Coventry, Shottery, Newton Aycliffe and finally Alcester. David describes his life with Hilary and their three sons with amusing stories of parish life interspersed with illustrations of formidable ecclesiastical personalities and ordinary parishioners, and not forgetting that part of pastoral life centred on baptisms, weddings and funerals.

ISBN: 978-1-85858-341-9 • PRICE £11.95

Available from:
History Into Print,
56 Alcester Road,
Studley, Warwickshire,
B80 7LG.

www.history-into-print.com